The Lightworker's Guide to Getting Started

Amy Scott Grant
Terry Robnett, RN

with contributions from
Jennifer Ripa and Lady Roxanna

Liberto Press
Castle Rock, CO

Published by Liberto Press
Castle Rock, Colorado, USA
© 2018 Amy Scott Grant and Terry Robnett, with contributions from Jennifer Ripa
and Lady Roxanna (Roxann Pool)
Book cover, design, and production by LibertoPress.com
Photograph of Amy Scott Grant by Andrew E. Grant
Photograph of Terry Robnett, RN by Tamara Muñoz
Photograph of Jennifer Ripa by Gina Sierra
Photograph of Lady Roxanna by Jo Hughes

Although the author and publisher have made every effort to ensure that the information in this book was correct at press time, the author and publisher do not assume and hereby disclaim any liability to any party for any loss, damage, or disruption caused by errors or omissions, whether such errors or omissions result from negligence, accident, or any other cause. Please remember to drink plenty of water when performing or receiving any kind of energy work or healing.

ISBN: 978-0-9974466-3-0

First Liberto Press printing, May 2018

Dedication

This book is dedicated to all our guides, seen and unseen.
Thank you for your guidance, your wisdom,
and your relentless love of us.

Thank you to each budding Lightworker
who is brave enough to take his or her next step.
You are the very reason we created this book!

Table of Contents

Introduction

Greetings and salutations! If you've picked up this book today, it's likely you've either just recently discovered the hidden world of energy, or you're now ready to discover what part you'll play in it. You may be feeling excited or apprehensive or overwhelmed (or all of the above). Please know that whatever you're feeling right now is just fine.

We've all been there. The day we realized we were "different" and for most of us, our first thought was, "Aw, crap. What the heck is this B.S.?!" One day you wake up and realize you're meant for more than an 8-5 job and a mediocre relationship, and oh by the way, you've also got "special" abilities. This epiphany can be both exciting and alarming. Most of us have been through this cycle of:

discovery → denial → resistance → ultimately, acceptance

With acceptance comes the ability to thrive, despite our freakishly inexplicable talents.

But aren't you the lucky one? Because there were no "how to" books for Lightworkers when we each awoke to our gifts. By the way, whenever we say "we" in this book, we mean the four contributing authors: Amy Scott Grant, Terry Robnett, Jennifer Ripa, and Lady Roxanna.

Today, there are countless books about energy work, but these are often meant for those who already know what their gifts are, or what types of healing modalities they wish to learn or pursue. Where then is the instruction manual for the recently awakened who may be feeling overwhelmed, confused, uncertain, and timid? Where's the how-to guide for those individuals who are experiencing things so bizarre and personal, that they don't even know what to type into the Google search bar?

Enter this book, *The Lightworker's Guide to Getting Started*. It's like a for-dummies guide for people with strange gifts, but without the condescending title or the assumption that you are anything less than an intelligent human who just happens to find herself or himself wading into unchartered territory. This is new to you, and therefore, this resource has appeared in your life to help you navigate these new waters.

Here's what you **will** find in this book:

- ✓ Clear and easy to follow descriptions, suggestions, exercises, and concepts, peppered with true stories and insights
- ✓ A non-denominational guide to your next steps, even if you're not quite ready to call yourself a "Lightworker" or even if you don't yet know what that means
- ✓ Clarity, focus, and a natural progression through what feels extremely supernatural
- ✓ Plain language and a well-organized format that's easy to follow and fun to read
- ✓ A glossary at the end of the book where you can reference any unfamiliar terms
- ✓ Helpful perspectives and experiences from four very different professional Lightworkers

✓ Practical advice (as if from a trusted BFF) about what you're feeling, where that's coming from, and how to handle it
✓ Personal, relatable experiences and anecdotes from compassionate badass Lightworkers who've been in your shoes and survived
✓ Guidance, resources, and provocative "Food for Thought" questions designed to help you advance on your own personal journey into light. As you read this book, you'll learn some of the terms for what you're feeling and experiencing, which will allow you to probe further into the specific areas of Lightworking that interest you most. That way, you don't have to Google vague questions like "am I losing my mind?" and "WTF is happening to me?"

What you **won't** find in this book:

- Any of us (the collective authors) trying to convince you that *our* way is the best way, or that there's only *one* true way to work with energy successfully
- Dogma, rules, restrictions, "shoulds" and "shouldn'ts," because we're not about to go "shoulding" all over the place
- Judgment, shaming, or authoritative dismissals of any kind
- Flowery, esoteric, or vague language
- A full, complete, or in-depth explanation of energy work, or of any specific modality. This book is an introduction to Lightworking and a guide to your next steps toward exploring and expanding your specific gifts and interests; it's not meant to tell you everything you need to know to set up shop as a specific type of Lightworker.
- Extensive self-promotion, upsells, cross-sells, or other marketing ploys.

As you read this book, you may become curious about some of us (the collaborative authors). The **About the Authors** section at the back of this book will give you more information about each of the contributing authors, including some free gifts, and will show you how to connect with us personally and professionally.

You can also meet the authors and a number of very cool like-minded peeps (from beginners to advanced) in our private Lightworker's Guide community:

TheLightworkersGuide.com

NOTE: Despite the best efforts of our editors, proofreaders, and beta readers, this book still contains some grammatical errors. Some of these were intentional. Amy and Terry's goal in writing this book for you is not to win a Newbury award (though admittedly, we wouldn't turn it down if it were offered to us). Rather, the intention is to provide you with the knowledge and understanding necessary to progress from uncertainty and confusion into your path as a Lightworker. Therefore, whenever it would have been awkward to rewrite a sentence without a dangling preposition, we chose not to. (See what we did there?) We trust you will find this book enjoyable nonetheless.

Now let's move forward together and explore your next steps in this wacky and wildly rewarding world we call "Lightworking."

With love, light, and badassery,

Amy & Terry

Chapter 1:

Oh No! Seriously?!

"I think I'd like to be an empath, or an intuitive, or a psychic healer," said no one ever. Being a Lightworker isn't so much something you choose as something that chooses you. Most of us who are chosen feel a lot of resistance to accepting our role as a Lightworker. But perhaps we should first lay some groundwork here and clarify exactly what we're talking about.

What the Heck is a "Lightworker" Anyway?

Webster's Dictionary defines "Lightworker" as—oh wait, that's right. It doesn't define it at all, because "Lightworker" is not *in* the dictionary. And yet, the term is fairly commonplace among all walks of energy workers and nontraditional healers. Put simply, *a Lightworker is one who works with energy toward a positive end.*

If that sounds a bit vague or generalized, think about it this way.

How would you define "food"? Perhaps: "a substance one eats." That short and sweet phrase defines this broad term, but without going into the finer details of the difference between pizza and chocolate soufflé', and without naming all the different styles and nationalities of food, or how to balance flavors, or how to cook. Lightworking is as vast and varied as food, and in many cases, just as enjoyable. Certain styles and methods will appeal to you more than others, which is wonderful because there are plenty of options to explore. By the time you're finished reading this book, you'll know what you're most interested in, and where to find more information about the Lightworking flavors that most intrigue you.

What Do Lightworkers Do?

You may know Lightworkers who consider themselves empaths, clairvoyants, energy workers, Reiki masters, intuitive healers, past life regression specialists, spiritual coaches, chakra balancers, or any other variety of names and labels. What all of these individuals have in common is their desire to raise the human consciousness through working with subtle energies. There's another common term you won't yet find in an ordinary dictionary. "Subtle energy" refers to the realm in which Lightworkers operate. Have you ever gotten "a weird vibe" from someone or some place? You were likely picking up on the subtle energy of the person or environment. You're accessing subtle energies when you sense someone's aura, or feel their feelings, or use a pendulum, or access your intuition, or work with the chakras, or perform a healing, or any other form of Lightworking.

Just as there are countless ingredients to choose from and a myriad of different ways to cook food, there are as many ways to work with subtle energies as a Lightworker. You might want to grab a snack, because I have a feeling this food-to-Lightworker analogy is going to keep popping up as we continue.

Terry: Delivering Messages and Saving Lives

It wasn't until I was in my 30s after having a serious meltdown where I wanted to stop the globe and get off that I actually came to grips with the fact that I am a Lightworker. I started to meet and spend time with like-minded people. It was then that I learned Reiki and became a master healer. I had the most amazing experience I will never forget while doing Reiki on another student. I could see inside her physical body and I saw that she was pregnant. But she did not know it, and when I asked her about it she was in complete denial. Spoiler alert: the pregnancy was later confirmed.

I had another experience with another student where a message came through very strongly. This was the first time something like that had happened to me and I didn't want to look stupid, so I resisted saying anything. What if I was wrong? What if they got mad at me? What if I gave them erroneous information that wound up doing more harm than good? But the urge to convey this message felt so strong it was like a pitchfork ready to poke my backside if I didn't deliver. I finally surrendered and the message turned out to be wildly accurate. This incident was so validating, it catapulted me to dive in deeper to learn all I could about the spiritual world and how it works, and as a result, I started using Reiki as much as I could. Just prior to all of this, I had gone through a midlife career change, went back to school, and became a nurse.

Once I became a Reiki master, I knew I was a healer. I was able to use Reiki selectively with permission from my emergency room patients. Once I had a patient who almost died from internal bleeding. I asked his permission to give him energy healing and he quickly agreed because he thought he was going to die. Two weeks after this event, he and his wife brought a huge basket of goodies to my nursing unit to thank me for saving his life. He was convinced that the energy healing he received had spared his life.

Even after all these experiences and many more, I still had difficulty coming to grips with what to do and make of all of this. Who could I share this with? What would people think? Are there other people like me? Am I just crazy?

Why Do Lightworkers Exist?

Lightworkers are here to bring in more light and divine awareness, allowing us to achieve higher levels of vibrational energy and consciousness. Right now, there's an upwelling of Lightworkers because as humans, we are currently undergoing some major transitions and elevations of consciousness. In other words, huge shizzle is going down in our Universe, and we need Lightworkers to guide us and support us through this transition. Put simply, more and more people are waking up to the idea that there's more to life than getting a good job, paying your rent, making your relationship work, and putting in your time until retirement. Many Lightworkers believe that by bringing in more light and raising consciousness, we will be able to find peace as well as solutions to some of the more daunting problems and issues we've created as a human race.

Lady Roxanna: You're a Cleaner.

My best friend Sarah came to visit me in New Orleans, and I stayed with her in the French Quarter. One day as we were out people watching, we walked around some of the more famous tourist attractions, such as Pirate's Alley, St. Louis Cathedral, and Jackson Square. As we walked and enjoyed each other's company, I noticed a funny pattern. When certain people walked near me, I abruptly started to sneeze and cough, even though I had been totally fine before they got near me.

When I mentioned it to Sarah, she turned to me and said, "You are a cleaner." "Okay, I thought. I'm a cleaner. I wonder what that means?"

That evening, we were behind St. Louis Cathedral where the view was just gorgeous and the moon was full. A photographer was all set up to take pictures of the scene. As we got closer, Sarah leaned toward me and said, "There is a negative entity on him and you are going to clean him." I thought this was interesting, given that I didn't know what a "cleaner" was, or how I was supposed to do this. But I trust Sarah, so I figured either she would tell me or I'd know what to do, so we continued walking toward the photographer. But as we got close to him, he suddenly turned and hightailed it the other way, leaving his camera and tripod still in place! Sarah laughed and said, "Apparently he changed his mind and didn't want to be cleaned." I was amazed and fascinated. These kind of odd occurrences continued the rest of the night, with me coughing and sneezing the more energy I (unknowingly) cleaned off of people. When I went home, my energy was so wonky, it took me two weeks to recover. I took quite a few salt baths, but it was still two weeks before I felt normal again. Today, I know how to protect my own energy so that I don't become negatively affected by the work I do to "clean" the energy of others, but back then it was all so new to me that I didn't really have a handle on what was going on, I just noticed that I was oddly coughing and sneezing. Now I know to pay attention when something unusual like that happens.

Why Me? Why Now?

Have you ever eaten a meal with someone who turned up their nose at what you were eating? We're reminded of a scene from the movie *My Big Fat Greek Wedding* where our young Greek heroine (Toula) tries to sit with the cool kids in the school cafeteria. The cool kids are eating their white bread sandwiches but when Toula opens the lunch her mother has packed for her, they gape at her in astonishment. "It's moussaka," Toula explains. The girls turn mean as they laugh and tease her, "You're eating *moose caca?*"

Yeah, the idea of telling people you're a Lightworker can feel as bad as that...times a million. You might be worried and wondering now:

> What if people think I'm a freak?
> What will my parents say?
> My _____ (church, religious family, friends, coworkers, employer, clients, etc.) will not understand this.
> I can't talk to anyone about this.
> Am I losing my mind?
> People will think I'm crazy.
> Why is this happening to me?
> I didn't sign up for this.
> Why now? This is terrible timing.
> My partner will dump me.
> What will other people think?
> This feels like an awful lot of responsibility.
> Is this a midlife crisis? (But what if you're only 32?)
> What if I attract some bad juju?
> I've got too much on my plate to deal with this right now.

We can assure you, whatever you're feeling right now is fairly common for Lightworkers who are just discovering they're different from other people. At this point, you may not see the many benefits of your unique potential, and you may perceive whatever makes you "different" as more of a burden than a blessing.

Jen: Go Away, Ghosts

*When I was a child, I communed with nature a lot. My best friend Meg and I would climb high in pine trees and sway with the wind. The trees had messages for me that I would relay to my friend and she would call me "nature girl." But looking back on my childhood, I would say I was more empathic than intuitive. I **felt** more than I **anticipated.** I could keenly read my* *parents' and siblings' emotions and sought to balance the often turbulent energy in the house.*

Being able to move energy was difficult to deal with while I was growing up. If I flipped on a light switch when I was angry, the light bulb would instantly burn out. I was inadvertently sending too much energy into the circuit, which burned out the bulb. My mother became aware that I was doing this and scolded me to stop creating hassles.

There was a ghost of a little boy in the house I grew up in. My brother Jay could see him and I knew he was there. When I would get home from school and let myself in through the garage, the sound of a child's footsteps running across the top floor always accompanied the turning of the key in the lock. The two sounds always went together. I remember seeing a ghost in the corner of my room when I was about seven or eight years old. It was the ghost of an adult man, and I would ask it to go away.

One of the houses I rented in college was quite haunted. Every morning, the basement lock would be opened even though it had been locked when my roommates and I went to sleep the night before. That was a particularly mean and troublesome ghost. I lived in that house my senior year and had travelled to India two years prior. During this learning abroad trip, my classmates and I had the good fortune to study yoga with T.K.V Desikachar. As a result, I had constructed a sacred altar in my room that included a framed photo of his father Sri Krishnamacharya.

In the mornings, I would practice yoga and meditate in front of the altar. Many days when I arrived home from class, the photo of Sri Krishnamacharya would be off of my altar and on the floor right in front of the doorway. Some days I accidentally kicked it before I noticed it there. Even today, I feel creeped out to think about it.

You Are Not Alone

Knowing that ghosts, guides, or other forms of entities exist may provide little comfort if you feel alone, lost, and confused right now. While you may be feeling as though you've got no one to talk to about your new discoveries, we can assure you with complete confidence and certainty that *you are not alone*. Countless other individuals are currently going through the same thing that you're going through, and whatever you're experiencing is far less wackadoo than you may think.

Every day, more and more people are waking up to discover they can do things that don't seem "normal." Individuals just like you are blowing out lights with the flip of a switch, seeing entities that aren't flesh and blood, knowing things that they have no explanation for knowing, and feeling like they're supposed to do *something* to help people, and to make a positive difference in this world. Like you, many of them feel confused, frightened, and uncertain where to begin or which step to take next.

We now urge you to consider that you are here now, reading *this* book, because you are ready to take your next step. Learning you're a Lightworker can feel like a confusing burden at first, but we assure you, it's an amazing journey and a precious gift. Don't crawl back under the covers or wish you'd taken the blue pill instead of the red. Instead, trust that this is your time to grow and to shine, and you're in good hands right now. Plus, Wonderland is far more interesting and rewarding than a lifetime of sleepwalking.

Amy: No Mom, I Didn't See the Devil

When I was a kid I knew things, but I couldn't explain how or why I knew them. I don't mean I was a smart-ass (although I kind of was. Still am, actually.). I often knew unusual or important or secret things, which surprised the adults in my life.

I remember going to my first Chinese restaurant at the age of five or six. My family was floored to watch me use chopsticks with ease, and when my mother asked me, "Where did you learn how to use chopsticks?" I casually shrugged and replied, "I don't know, I just picked it up somewhere." The whole table burst out laughing, though I had no idea why.

Eventually, I noticed the adults' sideways glances and nervous laughter every time I joined "grown-up" conversations, and it soon became evident that I was different. I soon realized that other people were not as comfortable with my insights as I was, so I tried to blame it on my imaginary friend, Chookel. (My brothers teased me incessantly about the name, pronounced "chew-kull," but what could I do? Sure, I would have liked "Jennifer" just fine, but when she first showed up, she said "Hi, I'm Chookel" and that was that.) But news of an imaginary friend who told secrets and taught me interesting things wasn't well-received.

Then one day around the age of nine, I was playing quietly in a huge cardboard box that had probably housed a new sofa or refrigerator (a fact you can only appreciate if you grew up poor, or lived across the street from a furniture store, or like me— both) when I saw a person who simply wasn't there. It appeared to be a teenage boy around my brother's age. He was wearing a football style jersey, exactly like one my brother owned, except my brother's was green and this guy's was red. When this guy opened the box he looked as startled to see me as I was to see him. Then he vanished. I climbed out of the box and looked around. "Hello?" No one answered. I walked into my dad's office and found both my parents there. "Who's here?" They exchanged their customary look of shock and horror and said, "No one is here, why?"

"I just saw someone, and I wanted to know who it was." I described what I had seen and where, and asked if maybe it was one of my brother's friends. My parents stared at me wide-

eyed and I will tell you what my mother said, so long as you promise not to judge her for it. Today, I'm certain she was stunned and scared and spooked as hell and didn't know what to say. Being an upstanding Catholic woman, she blurted out what must have been the first thing that popped into her head, which was this:

"Maybe it was the devil come to take you."

Now it was my turn to look shocked. Mom continued, "Well, you were laying in that box, maybe he thought it was a coffin and you were dead and he came to take your soul."

Despite the fact that I'd never seen any depiction of the devil that involved a teenaged boy in a red football jersey, my parents' reaction freaked me out enough that I shut down my intuition and didn't dare to open that particular Pandora's box again until well into adolescence.

I also stopped playing in cardboard boxes.

After Discovery Comes Denial, Resistance, and Acceptance

Perhaps a friend recommended this book and as you're reading, you're thinking to yourself, "I have no idea why she wanted me to read *this* book." Yet, you can't seem to put it down. If that's the case, you may still be in a stage of denial at this point. And that is fine! We're not here to convince you of anything, only to serve as helpful and experienced guides who have been in your shoes. Keep reading, and perhaps someday, you will call upon your stored memories of this book and these words will serve you. If not you, you may be able to help someone else who is in the process of discovering their own abilities.

More than likely, the fact that you're reading this now indicates that you're either in a state of resistance, acceptance, or ping-ponging back and forth between the two.

We Lightworkers often use the term "resistance" to refer to the energy a person exerts in order to avoid facing some certain Truth about themselves. Make no mistake about it, it requires a huge amount of energy to resist your truth. Waking up every day and doing work that's no longer fulfilling or staying in a relationship that's no longer satisfying; hanging out with people who are toxic for you; pretending you're not as magnificent as you really are because you're afraid of what that means—all of these are exhausting forms of resistance that cause you to feel fatigue and a lack of enthusiasm and joy. In many cases, prolonged resistance can result in physical illnesses and conditions. How often do you get sore throats or coughing fits? These are most often a result of refusing to speak your truth.

Terry: The Toilet Went Kaboom

My first memorable and inexplicable experience happened when I was about fourteen. I was at my friend's house and a lot of people were inside and out during the day. While I was in the house, I saw a long haired brunette female in a long white night gown float across the hall from the bathroom to a bedroom. I thought it was one of the girls who lived there. I ran down the hall to look but then saw nothing. I brushed it off as my mind playing tricks on me. Later that evening I used that same bathroom and while washing my hands, I heard what sounded like a loud explosion. Suddenly, the porcelain toilet bowl had a huge hole in the side of it as if someone had blasted it with a shotgun. Shockingly, nobody heard it and no one was even near the hall or the room.

After sharing this experience with my friend, she admitted that the previous owner had died in the house and that her house was haunted. It was during this time of my life that a lot of inexplicable things began to happen, and life grew more frustrating. I was intrigued but needed to understand what was happening to and around me.

We can understand if you feel resistant to being a Lightworker. No one wants to spend their paycheck replacing blown out light bulbs, or blowing up their friend's toilet (in the literal or figurative sense), or having their mother think they're dabbling with the devil. But on the other side of this resistance lives a whole new world teeming with excitement and peace and joy and possibility, and it's a world into which you have been called. Believe it or not, there's far less effort in accepting your role as a Lightworker and exploring what that means, and we can assure you, this is the most rewarding work you'll ever do.

Jen: What a Dumb Gift

Initially, I wasn't willing to trust the process and all I wanted was to go back to a lifestyle where what I did "fit in a box." One of my early gifts was to help people to hear their intuitive voice. I remember thinking to myself, "What a dumb gift. Why does THIS have to be my gift?" I wished I had chosen the path of being a doctor or an Olympic gymnast, two careers I had deeply considered as a child. Those paths make sense to people. Everyone knows what they are. Why does my gift have to be so weird and stupid and hard to explain? Consequently, I pursued training to become a health coach so that I could coach people about very concrete rational things such as diet, water intake, sleep habits, and stress management. Ironically, I attracted female clients who felt dead on the inside, needed a new direction in their life and wanted a deeper connection with their intuition. Of course!

In the next chapter, we're going to look at some of the different types of Lightworkers and start thinking about your specific gifts. In the meantime, take a few minutes to answer these Food for Thought questions. Nom nom nom.

Chapter 1 Food for Thought

1. Jot down anything you're feeling right now, perhaps about being a Lightworker, the stories you just read, or life in general. Try to avoid judgment and just capture the essence of your feelings.

2. If you are experiencing any fear or apprehension, see if you can specifically name or list what you're afraid of here. Often, naming our specific fears can alleviate some of our tension.

3. How did you first notice you were different? What happened? When did you suspect you weren't like other people? It may be something that happened recently, or something from your childhood. Take a few minutes to remember and write it down.

4. Do you have feelings, thoughts, or opinions about the term "Lightworker"? If so, what's a more neutral word you could substitute instead, so that your progress through this book isn't inhibited? Some examples include intuitive, special, gifted, healer, unusual, empath, etc.

Chapter 2: What Kind of Lightworker Are You?

We hope you have that snack handy, because the food-Lightworker analogy is about to boomerang back. The world of Lightworking is vast and varied. It may help to think of the different specific techniques of energy work as ingredients, the groupings of types of work as flavor profiles, and the results as successful dishes.

For example, just as food can be served raw or cooked, energy work can be hands on or hands off. It can be performed in person or remotely (over the phone, or without the two individuals speaking at all). You can do it yourself, or you can have someone do it for you, or a combination of the two.

Just as each chef has their own cooking style and flair, so does each individual Lightworker. New flavor combinations are invented in restaurants all over the world every day, and new methods of working with energy are sourced daily as well.

Here is a nowhere-near-comprehensive list of just a few of the types of Lightworking:

> Acupuncture
> Akashic records
> Angel reading
> Animal communicator
> Astrologist
> Candle reading
> Card reader (angel, tarot, oracle, etc.)
> Chakra work
> Channel
> Chiropractor
> The "Clairs" (clairvoyant, clairaudient, clairsentient, etc.)
> Crystals
> Crystal ball
> Dowsing
> Dream interpretation
> Energy artist
> Energy healing
> ESP (Extra Sensory Perception)
> Feng Shui
> Intuitive
> Life coach
> Massage therapist
> Medical intuitive
> Meditation
> Medium
> Numerology
> Palm reading
> Past life reading/past life regression
> Psychic
> Psychometry
> Reiki master
> Scrying
> Shamanism
> Yoga

At the back of this book, you'll find a simple glossary that includes an extremely brief description of each of the above.

Remember, the purpose of this book isn't to teach you how to cook, it's simply to introduce you to food and to give you some ideas of what kinds of Lightworking cuisines and ingredients you'd like to explore and learn more about.

With so many choices, how can you possibly choose just one? Good news, you don't have to! Some Lightworkers prefer to stick with just one or two modalities, but many employ several, selecting tools from their arsenal as the situation or healing requires. Just as you notice which dishes seem appealing to you on a menu, certain types of Lightwork will likely draw your attention, and you might find that you'd like to expand your palette.

Ways to Play

There are many ways to play in the realm of Lightworking and energy work. Some methods (often referred to as "body work") involve hands-on healing and energy work, while other types can be just as effective without any physical touch whatsoever. Remote healing refers to energy work that is performed remotely (not face to face). This can include phone work, healing work via email or Skype, or even work that's performed without a conversation of any kind. Some Lightworkers specialize in emotional healing, helping to resolve emotional wounds or upsets, while other Lightworkers focus on physical healing (for example, medical intuitives). There are countless ways to work with energy to bring health, happiness, freedom, and healing.

In addition to many ways to play, there are also many ways to help. Here are just a few of the ways Lightworkers help people:

- To get clarity
- To connect with departed loved ones

- To gain closure
- To receive insight
- To make sound decisions
- To release fears, phobias, and limitations
- To help ghosts and entities so they can move on (and leave our space)
- To recover from addiction, betrayal, and loss
- To discover and expand their own unique gifts
- To live their purpose
- To clear a space of negative energy
- To remove blocks in relationships, finances, career, health, happiness, etc.
- To heal physical pain, illnesses, and conditions
- To heal emotional pain
- To expand their mind
- To believe in themselves
- To break negative patterns
- To shift and release limiting beliefs
- And so much more

Jen Helps Women Stop Underestimating Themselves

I love to coach and mentor women who underestimate themselves because there's nothing like seeing the light turn on in their eyes during a session. It dazzles me to hear a new lilt in their voices and to see more color in their faces. I love noticing the physical changes in clients after a session that indicate they feel happier and more alive. This brings me an indescribable feeling of joy.

My method of life coaching helps people to identify patterns of behavior and belief systems that are inhibiting progress or creating obstacles to a desired goal. We combine this with subtle body energy work to create a truly remarkable transformation. When a client comes to me with a deep angst and yearning for more, it is my job to help them dispel any misperceptions, so they can feel more freedom and spaciousness. This way, they can take inspired action toward the spirit within themselves that needs to be discovered and expressed.

Lightworkers adopt many names and descriptive titles for their work and their gifts. Some are commonly recognized (yogi, shaman, coach, Reiki Master, psychic, tarot card reader, medical intuitive, medium, etc.) and some are unique (Spiritual Ass Kicker, Soul Gardener, Whole Being Enhancement Specialist, Lady Roxanna, etc.). At some point soon in your Lightworker journey, you'll want to have a way to describe what you can do for people, and this is where a name or title becomes useful.

Lady Roxanna: Earth Angel

Part of my energetic job involves being an Earth Angel, which means I'm here to transmute negative energy on the planet. Have you ever looked at the stars and felt like you don't belong here? I have done that numerous times. As an Earth Angel, we are here to assist with the ascension of the planet, and are highly evolved spiritually. Some things we Earth Angels all have in common are intense dreams, being intuitive, being aware of past lives, energy healing, and being very empathic. We generally try to avoid crowds and anywhere the energy feels very heavy or draining. For me personally, going to the grocery store or any big box store is very trying, so I avoid it as much as possible. I usually get my husband to pick up as many items as possible, just so I don't have to go. Part of being an empath includes learning how to manage and mitigate circumstances, people, and situations that zap your energy.

Now if you're feeling like a super newbie in this conversation, here's some common ground. Lightworkers feel...**a lot.** But the more we talk, the more we find we feel many of the same things, even though the ways we express ourselves and move energy may be very different. Just as people all around the world eat, but their food and even their utensils may be very different. See if you can relate to any of these common Lightworker experiences:

- You may feel unique and different in your own special way. You may even feel misunderstood or like you don't belong here.
- You are instinctively drawn to help people, animals, and the environment, and may have a hard time saying "no" to requests for help.
- You are sensitive to other's needs and very in-tune and receptive to energy in any space you occupy. You are empathetic and empathic.
- You feel a sense of purpose or destiny. You might not be clear on exactly what it is, but you know it's something bigger than you.
- You are by nature a teacher and a healer in many ways.
- You naturally attract people in need and you give of yourself, expecting nothing in return.
- You may feel drawn to eat healthfully and live a healthy life.
- You love the outdoors, plants, animals, and the miracle of life.
- Unlike most, you don't fear death or dying.
- You have very warm (often hot) hands.
- You are a natural born leader and you want to effect positive change.
- You tend to view life as a glass half full instead of half empty.
- You are very intuitive and know things but don't know how you know.
- People seem to come to you for everything, acting as though you have all the answers.

Terry: The Teacher and Student of Life

I am grateful to have many gifts that have evolved and multiplied over the decades. I have sought out countless classes, certifications, books and courses on a variety of modalities such as Reiki, Tarot, Astrology, numerology, Human Design, and witchcraft, just to name a few.

Intuition and claircognizance (an inner knowing) have always come easily and naturally to me for as long as I can remember. When I achieved Reiki Master, I thought for sure that I had fulfilled my journey by becoming a true healer working as a nurse with a certification in Reiki healing. Boy, was I wrong! That was when the truly inexplicable things began. Over time, I developed the ability and learned how to manifest, be clairaudient, clairvoyant, clairsentient, read auras, do auto writing, channeling, telepathy, divination, and many more. New gifts and inexplicable events just kept coming after my Reiki attunements—sometimes harder and faster than I wished or wanted them to. I realized during this time that I had more of a bonded and connected relationship with God, the Angels, and my guides than ever before.

I am a Lightworker and my quest as a Spiritual Mentor and Healer is to help those who really want it. You know the saying, "Teach a man to fish?" Well, that's me: the teacher. My purpose is to live each moment smiling and happy, to be the beacon of light that inspires others, to motivate and help others help themselves, and to create a global environment that promotes love, healing, and balance. I love the idea of helping people make a difference in their lives.

Just as I had thought my journey was fulfilled after becoming a nurse then a Reiki Master, again I thought the same when I started my coaching business. Nope. These are all stepping stones to what lies ahead. I have so much to teach and yet so much more to learn! Over the years, I have learned to ride the tide and go with the ebb and flow of what faces me, while remaining open to receive how, when, and where it comes.

We are all still learning. We have become teachers and yet, we remain students. Energy is vast, complex, and exquisite. This wild ride as a Lightworker will challenge and shape you in so many ways, and perhaps the greatest challenge comes to those who wish to know everything, to become masterful. But the work continues, even for the wisest and most experienced among us.

Amy: Learning Until I Die

I will never stop learning, right up until I die. I've been a Spiritual Ass Kicker for over a decade now, and my guides continue to surprise and delight me. I have learned to roll with the punches, which is especially helpful during client sessions. I have no attachment to my own methods or creations; rather, my intention in every session is simply to do whatever work is most optimal for that session. Because I am open and without attachment to how it goes, or to what part I play in the process, I am able to facilitate rapid transformational results for my clients. And yet, the Universe continues to school me. In the last couple of years, I've learned how to write fiction novels, taken professional cooking classes, and become an accomplished painter. I then realized it was time to learn how to draw, and then I began to learn how to do custom machine embroidery. Currently, I'm learning how to write scripts for sitcoms and feature films, and considering whether or not I'd like to enroll in film school. Learning is one of my core values and I cannot imagine my life without it.

For now, don't worry about where you belong in this Lightworker puzzle or what specific role you may play in the advancement of the human race. (No pressure.) Instead, take some time to reflect on your unique abilities and think about what you might like to learn more about. Consider who holds a special place in your heart, because this will provide some insight as to who you'd most love to help. Give yourself permission to be a student and to learn and discover. Know that any choices you make right now are unlikely to be "forever" choices—for now, simply relax and enjoy the journey as your learning unfolds. But first, here's your Food for Thought questions before we move on to the next topic: exploration.

Chapter 2 Food for Thought

1. Which (if any) of the Lightworking methods mentioned on page 20 seem most appealing to you?

2. What kinds of readings or sessions (if any) have you personally experienced or received from other Lightworkers? For example, Reiki, tarot cards, palm reading, medium, medical intuitive, etc. Can you recall what you were feeling during each session? For example, were you nervous, comfortable, freaked out, reassured, fascinated, repulsed, validated, spooked, or something else entirely?

3. How does intuitive information usually flow to you? Do you see it? Hear it? Feel it? Know it? List all the ways your special abilities have made themselves known.

4. If you could ask your guides any question about your path as a Lightworker, what would you ask? (Please do not move on until you complete this question.)

5. Which Lightworking methods (from page 20 or other) would you like to learn more about?

Now let's hold the shared intention that your guides provide an answer to the exact question you wrote in number four above. It might be answered over the next few chapters, or in a delightfully unexpected way. Be open to that answer finding you.

Chapter 3:

Exploration

Isn't it fascinating how time seems to stand still whenever we're doing something we love? We the authors love to learn! When we immerse ourselves in the process of learning and exploring, hours pass—perhaps even years—as we happily absorb and amass new and exciting discoveries.

In talking with many Lightworkers, we have found this to be the case more often than not, especially in the early stages of our journeys. Exploring this modality leads you to that person, which connects to yet another rabbit hole, and on and on it goes. We have each taken a wild and meandering path that was anything but predictable, even for the most psychic among us.

Terry: Tapping into Vast Potential

During my exploration, I discovered that the potential for gifts and how to use them is unlimited! I could learn and master and manifest whatever I was open to. I also discovered that I am the only one who stands in the way of my success. If my mindset was one of failure or negativity, then guess what? That's exactly what I would get! Hmm, imagine that. The law of attraction means like attracts like.

It has always been important to me to become skilled and masterful at whatever I went after. If there was a certificate, credentials, or some kind of acknowledgment, then I wanted that behind my name as proof that I AM masterful at it. However, I have come to discover that all those things are NOT proof and NOT needed. Hell, anyone can yank a certification off the internet these days. What really brings me the most personal satisfaction is delving into each gift and tapping into our vast potential.

The journey itself is so valuable and what could be more important than investing in your future and—not to freak you out, but we're going to say it anyway—the future of life on our planet? Yes, it requires time and often money and effort and other resources. Yes, while we're in the space of discovery we're rarely able to slow down long enough to appreciate its miraculous nature. Yes, it all feels like it's taking a long time and costing us a lot and can't we just fast forward already and get to the enlightenment part?

But, as the lyrics to "Cat's in the Cradle" suggest, wisdom comes with age, not with impatience. We're gonna have a good time then, aren't we? Perhaps you can learn from our past and enjoy this ride, having yourself a good time right here and right now. Follow the intuitive prompts you're getting, even when your logical brain is flipping out and saying, "We're gonna pay *how much* for this mentoring program? Jeez, that's more than my car is worth! Speaking of, how are we gonna pay the car note?"

Yes, we've all been there. And in hindsight, we wouldn't change one single step of it, because we wouldn't be the leaders we are today if we hadn't made all the choices we did, in order to get to this point. Don't cheap out on your own self development. This journey isn't about speed or frugality or a finish line; it's truly about the journey itself.

Jen: The Beginnings of Exploration

Upon arriving at college, I found a spaciousness and freedom to explore who I was that I'd never experienced before. Having been raised in a strict, hard-working, Irish Catholic family, my opportunities to contemplate metaphysics had felt very limited. I began to explore Eastern philosophical traditions, primarily Buddhism. I studied abroad in India, and this is when my mental framework was allowed to gradually shift away from a sin/punishment perspective to an obstacles/overcoming obstacles perspective. The liberty to see myself as something other than "a sinner" allowed me to ask, "What is God? How can I connect with God? How much of my own consciousness can I actually shape?"

After college, I went the corporate route, married my high school sweetheart, and we started a family. After a devastating miscarriage, I decided to do something meaningful for myself.

I enrolled in a 200-hour Kundalini Yoga Teacher training and that's when things in my life really started to change. I began practicing yoga every day, and became the lightest, freest, and happiest I had been since I was very young.

Kundalini Yoga opened up the reality to me that we are energetic beings having human three-dimensional experiences. The training and the daily practice helped me understand that the soul is the pilot and the ego/personality is designed to be the co-pilot through life. I began to see auras occasionally, would intuit my children's thoughts and feelings more easily, and began to see myself as a healer. I started studying Sat Nam

Rasayan, the healing branch of Kundalini Yoga, and could sense very subtle energetic shifts.

The intensive Kundalini asana and meditation practices burned through layers of guilt, self-hatred, shame, and self-blame, and allowed the inner light of my true being to shine. I would never have called myself an intuitive at that point, but for certain, I was finally happy.

During this exploration stage, we encourage you to look into many different ideas, concepts, and modalities, to discover which ones resonate with you the most. In Chapter 2, we touched on some of the different types of energy work, and hopefully, at least a couple of those sparked your interest. You can begin by searching YouTube for instructional-style information, or search online for Lightworkers who specialize in these modalities.

We the authors of this book each work with several different forms of Lightworking, so check out our bios in the About the Authors section at the end of this book and see what vibes with you. Look at many resources and dive more deeply into those that feel most appealing to you. Now probably isn't the time to drop twenty grand on a certification program, especially if it's the first or second website you've looked at. Rather, this step is about investing time in your discovery, reading books and finding teachers, in order to gain a clearer understanding of where you're drawn to go next.

Amy: Half a Million Dollars

As a young child, I remember hiding in my sister's closet trying to move a pencil with my mind. I was certain it could be done, I just couldn't figure out how to do it. Who would I ask? Everyone I knew was Catholic. In hindsight, it's shocking that I never asked Chookel how to do this stuff. Ah, but such is the plight of a fierce independent soul.

At the age of thirteen, a book about the power of the mind fell out the Universe and into my hands and that book saved my life from impending suicide. But eventually, I fell back into my old ways, not quite ready to delve into my gifts. In college, someone handed me a copy of Illusions *by Richard Bach and my mind was blown. Yeah, I know it's a fiction book, but is it, really? I was convinced anything in that book could happen, and that it could happen to me. Again, it expanded my mind in terms of what's really possible, but it didn't provide me with instructions on how to get there. Perhaps you felt the same way when you first saw the movie* The Matrix. *Okay, so there is no spoon. But* **how** *do I get the dang thing to bend without using force?*

When my husband and I decided to have kids, I knew I wanted to escape from the corporate grind, so we started looking for ways to work from home. Although our stint in network marketing was short-lived, it introduced us to some amazing teachers and concepts, and I began studying and testing the Law of Attraction (mind you, this was years before The Secret*). I hired coach after coach after coach and bought program after program, scooping up everything that said "YES" to me. My appetite was insatiable for learning about energy and the power of the mind. In about a decade's time, I spent close to half a million dollars on my own self-development and learning.*

Sure that sounds like a lot, but guess what? I can now bend a spoon, bend my mind, and a whole lot more.

Investing in Yourself

Consider our comparison of Lightworking to the world of food. If today you decided you wanted to learn how to cook, would you immediately enroll in the Culinary Institute of America (with an estimated cost of around $17,000)? Perhaps, but that wouldn't be the solution for most people. More likely, you would start by looking up some online cooking videos, reading a lot of cooking blogs (So. Many. Cooking blogs!), and watching cooking shows on the Food Network. Then, once you found a chef, or a cuisine, or a style of cooking you resonated with, you'd probably buy a few cookbooks and start watching cooking shows more selectively. Once you felt you had a basic understanding of the techniques, then you might feel ready to buy some ingredients and cooking tools and try out the methods in your own kitchen. You would experience some successes and some failures, which would prompt you to seek more guided training. This is when you'd sign up for local cooking classes or attend a cooking retreat or workshop. Once you were certain where you wanted to specialize or focus, that's when you'd likely want to consider certification and a more intensive study.

The process is similar for Lightworker exploration. Sure, some Lightworkers have discovered Reiki (or a similar method), gotten attuned and certified, and then never explored any other modality. Admittedly, we're seeing very little of this today. Most Lightworkers start with one modality, work it through to mastery (or to the point where it's no longer appealing to them), and then branch out into a different modality. Many Lightworkers continue to add to their skillset, and/or source their own methods by simply remaining open and receptive to whatever intuitive guidance they receive.

Amy: Nope, No Thank You

It was only when I grew frustrated with what I perceived to be the clunkiness and inefficiency of other Lightworkers' methods that I started sourcing my own methods, without realizing that's what I was doing. Frankly, I was impatient and impetuous, and I wanted everything to happen more quickly, so that's when I started to improvise. Can't you just imagine me, arms folded and stamping my feet in frustration like a child who was just denied candy?

A Lightworker once taught me how to do a cord cutting. I did it, and immediately felt better. Then, an hour later, I was upset again. I called her back and said, "Hey, what gives? This frustration is back." She told me, "Oh honey, you might have to cut that cord a thousand times before you're totally free from this person." Nope, no thank you. I figured, if we are all truly made of energy, then there's got to be a way to make a clearing **permanent.** *So that's what I set out to do, and that's what I still do today: once and done. Because I don't know about you, but I got a lotta crap to clear and I can't be doing any of it one thousand times.*

Truly, I didn't realize I was anything special until one of my coaches told me in an awestruck voice that she'd never seen anyone do the things I was doing, much less as fast as I was doing them. "Hmmm," I thought to myself. "Well, isn't that interesting."

At some point, a mentor or coach becomes essential to your journey. There are Lightworker coaches (like our own author Terry Robnett) who specialize in working with newbies, helping you to open up to your intuition and explore different modalities. There are Lightworkers who can mentor you in a specific healing modality. There are Lightworkers like our own author Amy Scott Grant, who can help you to get unstuck, to clear your own blocks and fears, and whatever is keeping you from moving forward. If you're like most Lightworkers, you will have many mentors and coaches throughout your journey. The more you learn to trust your intuition, the easier it will be to find your next guide to assist you through each stage of transformation.

Terry: The Value of an Experienced Mentor

From as far back as I can remember, I have been enamored by magic, ghosts, aliens, and the inexplicable. All my favorite shows, movies, and books growing up and even to this day involve witchcraft, magic, ghosts, and fantasy. Like a lot of kids/teens growing up, I dabbled in magic, Ouija, manifesting, and witchcraft (just to name a few). Looking back, I sought out countless modalities over time just to see what vibed with me and I discovered that I learned better and faster with hands-on training. Attempting to discover your own learning style and being patient with the learning period can be frustrating without a teacher, coach, or mentor to guide and support you. Without guidance, it can be very difficult to keep an open mind and trust the process, because you will run into so many inexplicable things.

Just like life, I think it's impossible to have knowledge without education and/or experiences to learn from. It's even better if you have a mentor; someone to guide you through the hard crap. Nowadays, you can find help and connection via countless groups on Facebook, local meet ups, social media, and even through apps on your phone. Resources are easy to find in this day and age. One book that helped push me forward when I was at a serious crossroads was Real Magic *by Dr. Wayne Dyer.*

During this period of exploration, give yourself the time and space for discovery. Grant yourself permission to meander and explore. For many of us, the entire path is not illuminated at once; only the next step or the next couple of steps are made clear at a time. Therefore, don't focus too hard on what lies ahead; just begin the discovery process. Consider your own personal learning styles. Do you enjoy reading? If so, start searching online or meander the aisles at your local library or bookstore and see what jumps out at you. Books are an excellent place to start.

Lady Roxanna: Thank You, Granny

My granny's shelves were filled with books on Astrology, Hypnosis, and all sorts of unusual topics, and I read them all.

All my life, I have been a student of life, and Granny's many books gave me a great start. I love to study and have spent my life acquiring knowledge and hopefully, wisdom.

In addition to my spiritual studies, I hold two Bachelor's degrees: one in Nursing and the other in Psychology. I am a Reiki Master Sensei. I adore crystals and gems and have received certifications as a Certified Crystal Healer (CCH) and Advanced Crystal Master (ACM). I am a certified Sacred Activations Practitioner. I have completed numerous studies in Feng Shui, Numerology, Aromatherapy, and many others, all in my quest to learn as much as I can and understand energy.

What I have learned is there is always more to know and you learn to work with it and tweak it as you go. I am an I AM Angelic Miracle Healer. I began studying this after my father died in 2010, shortly after I returned home from a trip to England. I work with clients one-on-one using the help of the angels to provide the best healing for each and every client. I also provide email readings and chakra scans. Since my father died, I have been studying mediumship and providing readings for friends, family, and some clients. Mediumship is quickly becoming one of the services I most frequently offer, as it provides consistently excellent results. Thank you, Granny for helping me explore and begin my path at such an early age.

Perhaps you learn best by observing and watching someone else. If so, YouTube or Vimeo would be your best bet, as well as specific Lightworkers' vlogs and websites. Are you an auditory learner? Check out the Lightworker podcasts on iTunes and BlogTalkRadio (NOTE: also search metaphysical, energy healing, and spiritual healer). Check out Audible for books on tape. Many healers, including some of the authors of this book, have audiobooks, audio healings, and audio training programs available through our websites.

Jen: Learning to Be Steady

The times that I was most blocked from my intuition were the ones in which I didn't want to hear bad news. I continue to open to my intuition every day and with each client. I get more and more comfortable hearing or sensing difficult news and potentially tragic situations. The loss of my son to cancer and my healing journey since have allowed me to be okay with being steady for clients during very difficult times. A coach can only take a client as far as they themselves are willing to go, and being willing to go into the depths of darkness that life has to offer provides a great deal of impartiality. I now know that this impartiality is the true key to being a helpful and valuable coach.

Give Yourself a Gift

Now is a time to be patient with yourself and keep an open mind. Sometimes the very methods or teachers that feel repulsive to you hold a certain lesson or message that will serve you. Be open and receptive, and be willing to explore with the eyes and heart of a child. You just never know what will come forth from this part of your journey.

In the meantime, you can connect with all types of Ligthworkers from many walks of life (plus the four authors) here in our Lightworker's Guide private community:

TheLightworkersGuide.com

Why not take a minute now to join, before you move on to the Food for Thought?

Chapter 3 Food for Thought

1. Have you ever felt as though you were the light in the darkness? Take a minute to recall a few of the times that you felt this way and make notes here about how you handled it.

2. Do you find yourself on a constant path to elevate yourself (mentally, emotionally, spiritually, and/or physically)? If so, list all of the ways you elevated yourself (e.g., courses, books, retreats, conferences, workshops, etc.). Circle the ones that you feel made the biggest impact.

3. During your own exploration, what "gifts" (intuition, premonition, etc.) have you discovered about yourself so far? How do you feel about having these gifts?

4. Write down some modalities (Astrology, Numerology, Tarot, Angel readings, etc.) that are of the MOST interest to you, that you would like to research and learn more about. Circle the top three that feel most appealing right now.

5. What is it about each of these three modalities that feels most appealing to you?

Chapter 4: Did I Just Make that up?

For many Lightworkers, the biggest learning curve involves distinguishing between intuition and the brain. How can you tell if something is coming from Divine awareness, or if your Ego is jumping in to protect you from harm? How do you know whether it's intuitive guidance talking, or something your brain just figured out? What's more, if you don't yet know the difference, how can you trust that your "knowings" are actually coming from the Highest Good, rather than your brain or your Ego?

The short answer is: **it's a process.** Through practice, patience, and occasional validation, we each learn to trust the information we receive. The duration of this process varies from Lightworker to Lightworker, but it is most definitely part of the journey for all of us.

Terry: The Battle Between Brain and Intuition

Who knows how far back I started questioning myself about things I knew but didn't know how I knew? I just knew! When you're a kid, adults accuse you of making things up, having an overactive imagination, or talking to fantasy friends. This kind of conditioning often starts at birth, so when I began to experience things outside of the norm (whatever that is), I learned to protect myself by keeping quiet about what I knew.

As I got older, I began to question how and why I saw/heard/thought/felt/smelled/tasted/just knew things. I asked myself questions like: How does that happen? Where does that come from? Am I the only one experiencing this? Who am I to know things I have never experienced? Who can I talk to or share this with? The search for answers propelled me forward in my journey.

In the beginning, until a high level of trust is established, we tend to speak in disclaimers, like "this might sound crazy, but...." We'll dive into that more deeply in a later chapter. For now, let's examine this doubt, where it comes from, and how to eliminate it so you can trust your inner guidance more fully.

Doubt is defined as simply "uncertainty." Doubt in and of itself is not a bad thing. It can help protect you when someone is lying to you, and it can help prevent you from making terrible mistakes. But when we live in a state of perpetual doubt, we become paralyzed and unable to live fully and powerfully.

Trust Yourself First

Learning to trust your guidance and intuition is very closely linked to your level of self-trust. Self-trust refers to one's ability to value, rely on, listen to, and believe in oneself. Whether or not you trust yourself is a factor that carries influence all throughout your life. For example, your level of self-trust will affect:

- Your ability to make sound decisions
- Your peace of mind
- Your intuition and psychic abilities
- Your trustworthiness, as perceived by others
- Your relationships (How can you trust others if you can't trust yourself?)
- Your success level
- Your finances (It's difficult to make wise money choices if you don't trust those choices, and it's nearly impossible to become wealthy if you don't trust yourself with money.)
- Your satisfaction level
- Your ability to love and accept yourself

The core issue of self-trust seeps into all aspects of life and can be especially troublesome to budding Lightworkers. Self-doubt is the antithesis of self-trust, and unfortunately, self-doubt is pervasive. The person who doubts himself or herself cannot establish healthy, supportive, lasting relationships; cannot create a substantial level of wealth or success; and cannot grow and expand his or her intuition and abilities as a Lightworker. Self-doubt is like a dark cloud, following the person around, leaving him or her always expecting rain, but never knowing when the downpour will strike.

Where Does Self-Doubt Originate?

Essentially, we can track the origin of self-doubt back to one of three time periods. Self-doubt may have originated:

- In a past life
- In this life, but in the distant past (often beginning in childhood)

- In this life, brought about by an adverse turning point or series of events

Amy: But I Wasn't Eavesdropping

When I was a little girl, I was forever getting into trouble at home for knowing things I couldn't possibly have known. I was often accused of eavesdropping (which I only sometimes did). Later, when I was "out of the spiritual closet" in my thirties, my mother confessed to me: "We really didn't know what to do with you. We thought you were an alien from another planet."

Self-doubt grows with a compound effect. We've all made choices in life we're not necessarily proud of. We might go so far as to call them dumb choices (or worse). That is part of life—we all make mistakes. But sometimes, the consequences of these mistakes are grave and we have difficulty forgiving our erroneous choices. Other times, one bad choice can lead to an adverse event, which then snowballs into a series of bad choices, until we find ourselves deep in the quicksand of self-doubt. Here are a few examples.

An Example of Self-Doubt from a Past Life

Laura goes out of her way to please people. As an empath, she can't handle anyone crying in her presence. She feels an overwhelmingly strong need to comfort and appease, and she avoids conflict and confrontation at all costs. Laura often wonders if she's good enough. She needs constant validation, but that doesn't allay the self-doubt that bubbles up inside of her.

Laura will forego what she really wants (if she even knows what she wants) in lieu of trying to make someone else happy. She won't give someone the guidance she receives if it feels like bad news. She won't use her abilities to challenge someone to grow, because that feels extremely uncomfortable to Laura, and she doesn't want to upset them.

If we look into Laura's past lives, we would likely find evidence of a past life where Laura had great power and used it against people. She carries this burden into today's lifetime. This shows up as doubting her ability to make her own choices, because she doesn't trust herself with desire, power, and leadership. She sets out to please others in an unconscious way, to try to make up for the terrible past life things she's done.

Terry: Finally Free from the Vicious Cycle

For me, when this "knowing" from all my senses began, I just spoke my mind. I would share whatever came up. I would only get embarrassed or feel challenged when people adamantly disagreed or got analytical on me. Then I would feel like I had to defend myself, so I felt stupid and shut down. I have never liked confrontation, I mean, who does? Whenever this happened, I would second-guess myself about whether or not I really just made all that stuff up. All the doubts, fears, lack of confidence and knowing would come flooding in, causing me to seek approval to gain my own trust back. It was a vicious cycle and I'm so happy to be freed from it now!

An Example of Self-Doubt from This Life, but from the Distant Past

Oh, Jan. Jan's self-doubt stems from her **childhood,** when she always felt overlooked and overshadowed by her smarter, prettier, more popular sister Marcia. At some point, Jan decided that if Marsha got all the attention, it must be because Jan herself wasn't worthy of attention. Today, Jan's self-doubt limits her ability to thrive as a Lightworker, as she is always questioning whether the information she's receiving is accurate, valuable, or helpful. She doubts whether her gifts will even make a difference. Marcia, Marcia, Marcia!

An Example of Self-Doubt from This Lifetime, from a Recent Turn of Events

Mary was always a go-getter, and she had set up a pretty sweet life for herself. But one day, Mary's wonderful world shatters when she finds out her husband wants a divorce because he's in love with someone else. Then she gets laid off from her cushy job and suddenly finds herself facing a lot of simultaneous life changes. Next she finds out she's a Lightworker?! How can Mary learn to trust her intuition when her life seems to be falling apart?

Jen: Coaching Others Helped Me

When I first started working with clients, I suffered from fear of judgment. I was still working through my Catholic upbringing and having mental barriers around who could speak with the Divine and under what circumstances. Coaching others helped me become more comfortable with my ability to be in the flow of information. In the beginning, if I had a client with a Christian viewpoint or one who didn't believe in past lives, that would throw me off my game. I often stuttered and repeated the same information while waiting for new information to come through. Guidance flowed very slowly because my nervousness and judgment had either slowed it down or shut it off temporarily.

The Enemy of Intuition

Intuition refers to your inner knowing, your awareness of what's going on around you, and what's coming down the pike. The single biggest enemy of your intuition is self-doubt, because self-trust cannot exist where self-doubt is present.

If you don't trust yourself, you will find yourself unable to trust any information you receive intuitively. Instead, you'll have thoughts like:

- I think I'm making all this up.
- The other night I watched a documentary on this, so that must be where this is coming from.
- That can't be true, can it?
- Now that I know, what am I supposed to do about it?
- That doesn't make any sense.
- That seems very far-fetched/unreal.
- That seems like too great of a coincidence.
- No one will believe that/me.
- I've never in my life heard such rubbish.
- I don't know what that means.
- I'm just not getting enough info.
- I think I'll check with my pendulum again. And again. And again. And again. Oh wait, now the answer is changing. Oh no, now what?

Intuition is a powerful tool and asset, and one that can serve you in many aspects of your life. But when the waters are muddied by self-doubt, intuition can seem like an impossible dream. Here's something to consider:

Have you ever received an intuitive "hit" to do or say something, but ignored that hit? What happened as a result?

Amy: I Needed Answers

Remember I told you about the day I saw the guy who wasn't there and my parents freaked out? That's when I shut down my intuition until adolescence. But a funny thing happens when we deny our true nature, only it's not funny at all. We suddenly feel lost, confused, and uncertain. By the age of thirteen, I had made multiple suicide attempts, convinced that I did not belong in *this world. The idea of living life without being truly known or understood by another human being felt like too much for me to bear. I needed answers, and desperately fast. When those answers showed up in a miraculous way, I decided **not** to shut down my abilities again, but instead, to simply keep them private.*

If you're like most people, ignoring your intuition came back to bite you in the ass. Here are **seven simple tools to foster more self-trust** so you can listen to your intuition and keep your ass intact.

Method #1: Clear the Doubt

You can clear self-doubt, just like any other block or limiting belief. Regardless of where/when your self-doubt originated, you can be freed from that doubt, and it's actually easier than you think. If your abilities are still developing, work with another Lightworker to get cleared.

Method #2: Listen to the Nudges

One of the simplest (though not always easy!) ways to grow self-trust is to start listening to those intuitive nudges, without second-guessing yourself. Got a "hit" to take an umbrella even though the sky is crystal clear? Do it. Maybe you'll discourage a mugger who sees you walking around with a big ol' umbrella on a sunny day. BONUS: The more you listen, the more the Universe starts talking. In other words, you can expect your intuition to grow as a by-product of this.

Method #3: Use Truth Testing

Truth Testing is a great tool to help you learn to trust yourself. Hang tight, because we'll show you how to do it in this very chapter. Truth testing provides you with an objective method for testing to see what is true, so you don't have to worry about "is that real?" Yay, instant validation!

Jen: Doubt Stops the Flow

When I first started practicing on other people, doubt expressed itself as stopping. I would shut down information or stop asking questions when I felt insecure. I would look for logical explanations for information I received, and try to explain things in terms of what I already understood. I also remember having a lot of migraine headaches in the beginning. A knot would form in my stomach when the news was not good or the information involved a tricky topic that I didn't want to share.

Method #4: Relax

It sounds too simple, right? But the more relaxed you are, the easier it is to quiet that nagging voice of doubt inside your head. Meditate, take naps, go for relaxing walks, take bubble baths—whatever helps you to relax and unwind. The more relaxed you are, the less room there is for self-doubt, and the more space you give yourself for self-trust. Additionally, when you nurture and take care of yourself, you are reinforcing the idea that **you have value.** And when you feel you have self-worth, then self-trust is more likely to join the party, too.

Terry: I Was Magic

As a little girl growing up, I always knew I was different. I was convinced I was magic and could make things happen just with a thought. I remember my dad driving down the freeway in traffic and saying to me, "Terry, can you just wiggle your nose and make the traffic go away?" Little did I know, he was just playing into my magical fantasy, especially since I loved the show Bewitched. As far as the traffic was concerned, I'd set the intention and sometimes it would clear and sometimes it wouldn't. That was frustrating, but because I was young, it didn't fluster me as much as it would have as an adult. Back then I just figured, "Hmm.... I guess my magic isn't working today."

Method #5: Tap into Higher Consciousness

Sometimes, when it seems impossible to trust ourselves, it feels a bit easier to trust in a power that is higher/greater than ourselves. You can connect with it and draw energy and wisdom from it. You might call this higher power God, Spirit, the Divine, Bethany, or any other name you choose. Consider that you were created from a Divine Spark, which means you can tap into that inner spark and ask it to guide you.

Method #6: Break Negative Patterns

Here's a simple yet powerful method Amy calls the **Pattern Shatter.** In an instant, you can shatter a pattern by simply choosing a different action. For example, how do you normally respond to your own negative self-talk? What if the next time it happens, you simply interrupt the thought with "No!" or "Cancel that!" and then create a new, more positive, more supportive thought in its place? Try it and watch what happens.

Method #7: Associate with More Like-Minded Peeps

We can't help it—we wind up talking like, acting like, and thinking like the people we spend the most time with. If some of the people in your life are negative, then it might be time to upgrade your social circle. At this point in your journey, it's almost certainly time for you to meet and hang out with more Lightworkers.

A few of the benefits of hanging out with other Lightworkers include:

- Being able to practice on each other without judgment
- Receiving constructive feedback from someone who understands Lightworking and has gifts of their own
- Having an objective third-party to verify information you're receiving, which can provide validation which in turn builds confidence more quickly
- Having a support network of people who speak your language and appreciate what you can do

Lady Roxanna: I Know What I Felt

After my Reiki Master/Sensei level attunement in 2010, my best friend Sarah and I we were visiting some castle ruins in Bathe, England. I knew instantly when I stepped on a spot where something bad had happened. I got quite nauseous and my husband looked at me and said, "Are you okay?" The feelings intensified and I didn't get any relief until we were driving away from the castle ruins. A couple of days later we went to London. While on the Jack the Ripper tour, I could tell you when I was standing on the exact spot where a murder occurred. The absolute worst spot was The Tower of London. Outside wasn't really a problem, but inside, some areas made me feel extremely ill. There wasn't a trash can in sight, and the only window was four inches square. I desperately thought I was going to throw up! Luckily, I held it together and managed to get out without incident. Sure, some people might not believe me, but I know what I felt.

Fear Serves a Purpose

How can you know whether an underlying fear is guiding your actions and limiting your opportunities? Fear can trigger a flight-or-fight response, and while that might have been a primary survival tactic back in the caveman days, today we humans face many subtler, insidious fears on a day-to-day basis. Our tendency to respond to fear by running away (emotionally, mentally, or physically) can interfere with our role as Lightworkers. While fear seeks to protect us and keep us out of harm's way, intuition can also keep us safe, but with the added benefit of helping us expand into a bigger, more adventurous experience of life, as well as helping others and our entire planet.

You can likely recall a time in your life when you felt a certain nudge not to do something, and then later you felt relief when you were glad you had listened to that intuitive prompt. Learning to develop and listen to your intuition can provide you with invaluable guidance and direction in all areas of your life. But how can you tell whether it's your intuition guiding you toward saying no, or whether it's your fear stopping you from saying yes?

The Importance of Knowing the Difference

To make the best possible decisions and choices, you must be able to distinguish between an intuitive warning and a fear-based fight-or-flight response. Is it your fear that's causing you to hesitate about saying yes, or is it your intuition letting you know this isn't the right time or the right option for you?

Whenever you are faced with a choice or opportunity, and you're not sure if "no" is the right answer, consider the following three questions.

1. How does the choice feel?

If you feel a sense of urgency to say no, especially if there's no true deadline impending, then it's likely your fear that's driving you to decline. On the flip side, a truly authentic intuitive "no" typically won't budge, even when sales pressure is applied. A sense of urgency to say no and be done with the decision is likely fear-based, whereas a calm and relaxed "no, thank you," is more likely your intuition talking.

2. If you say "no" to this, are you moving *toward* or *away from* something?

Fear-based decisions usually move you away from something you don't want. In these situations, a fearful "no" helps you to avoid failure, feeling bad, or looking stupid. You're mitigating risk by avoiding what feels too scary—even if the thing that scares you is what you actually want. In contrast, an intuition-driven "no" typically leads you toward something you truly want.

3. Have you fully considered the implications of saying yes or no?

An authentic, intuitive "no" means you're not afraid to look at what you might be missing out on, or what could happen if you were to say "yes." But often, when a "no" is borne out of fear, little to no consideration has been given to the ramifications of either outcome. You could miss out on potentially amazing opportunities if you're quick to say no out of fear. Now that you know how to discern the difference, you can go forward to make smarter, calmer, more appropriate choices and decisions, without being ruled by fear.

Jen: Without Support, I Felt Judged

I had so much doubt in the beginning, and it showed up in so many ways! The most difficult part was the lack of support or approval from anyone in my life. My oldest son thought I was doing something evil by using a pendulum. My husband thought I was going a bit nuts. I didn't feel understood or supported in becoming an intuitive and in fact, I felt judged. When I started to delve into intuitive information directly, my only support person at that time was my coach (Amy Scott Grant).

Even today, my family doesn't get what I'm into or what my work is. But thankfully, my support network has grown tremendously. I have many friends, clients, and fellow healers who share my passion for Lightworking, and I'm very grateful for their understanding. However, lack of support was a huge challenge in the beginning.

Truth Testing is a powerful way to confirm and validate the information and insights you're receiving. For our four authors here, we have all relied heavily on truth testing at one time or another, especially when we were first exploring our Lightworking abilities. Truth Testing is a highly effective way to remove doubt, build trust with yourself, and learn to rely on your intuition and your guides.

Lady Roxanna: This Is Our Job

Clairvoyance was my strongest sense at first and it remains my fallback method. I see pictures in my mind or third eye. In the beginning, I would try to understand the images I was getting. Sure, there were a few times when I thought, "Did I make this up?" My spiritual teacher told me, "Trust what you get," and my angels have confirmed this as well. We all have angels and guides who are here to assist and protect us. I check in with my angels during readings and private sessions to assist my clients in the best way possible. My doubt was very short-lived and I quickly learned to trust whatever images I received.

Yes, there will be times when you read for someone, and they say they don't know what you're talking about, or that it doesn't mean anything to them. Your information could be spot on, but they just don't understand it yet or aren't ready to hear it. Don't worry because they will often remember something or figure it out later, although you won't get confirmation of this unless they contact you.

I have done many email readings, and unless the person asks a follow-up question, there's no way for me to know what they did with the information I provided. It's only our job to deliver the info to those who ask; it's not our job to know what they do or don't do with that info. This is why it is so important for us to trust our guides, and to use Truth Testing when we feel the need to validate information.

Truth Testing

Truth testing is a process used to verify and/or validate information. There are many reliable Truth Testing methods, but here is a taste of just one to help you get started: the pendulum. To become masterful at using a pendulum (remember how we said it helps to start with books?) get a copy of Amy's book *Pendulum Mojo,* available on Amazon.

The following introduction to the pendulum is excerpted from Amy's book *1-2-3 Clarity: Banish Your Blocks, Doubts, Fears, and Limiting Beliefs Like a Spiritual Badass.* If you're more the visual type (or highly impatient), check out Amy's YouTube channel for how-to videos.

> A pendulum consists of a string or chain with an object of weight on one end. In a pinch, most anything can serve as a pendulum: a pendant on a necklace, a cell phone charger, a digital camera, a piece of yarn and a washer, even a water bottle on a carabiner.
>
> Keep in mind, there is no power in the pendulum other than the power you give to it. Can you see it for what it is? It's just a piece of string with a dangly bit on one end. The power comes from your Highest Self, the part of you that is connected to all of life and everything in the Universe. Truth Testing with a pendulum consists of three steps:
>
> Step 1: Calibrate

Step 2: Phrase Your Question Mindfully

Step 3: Relax and Await Movement

Step 1: Calibrate

Once you are experienced with using a pendulum, you can hold it any old way you want but if you're a newbie, start out this way:

Sit up with your back straight and your feet uncrossed and flat on the ground. Pick up your pendulum with your dominant hand and bend comfortably at the wrist. Imagine the energy is coming off your hand and down into the pendulum, like a waterfall.

Keep your elbow down to keep your arm from getting tired. At first it can take a while until you get the hang of it and pick up speed. So for now, elbow down, and it's best while you're first learning to avoid resting your elbow on anything.

The dangly part of the pendulum should be even with the middle of your chest, so that your pendulum hangs about six to eight inches in front of your heart chakra. Relax your shoulder, your wrist, and your jaw. These are places where most people hold tension, and tension is just a form of resistance, and resistance is what stops you from being able to do energy work. Relax your jaw and this will remind you to release tension.

Remember, the pendulum can't do anything without a person, because the energy comes from the person, not the pendulum. If you have your shoulders scrunched up around your ears, how well do you think energy will flow through you? Relax. Breathe. Relax and breathe some more.

Now you can *calibrate,* to find out what your signs are. Calibration is fairly simple. You will ask three separate questions with a pause between each to check the direction of movement. It doesn't matter if your eyes are open or closed, but some people find it is easier to be patient when their eyes are closed as they wait for the pendulum to move. You can say the following calibration statements out loud or in your head:

Please show me a clear sign for "yes." Then wait for it to move and notice which way it's moving. If the direction is circular, notice whether it's clockwise or counter clockwise. Be patient and remain focused on the statement/question at hand; it can sometimes take several minutes if this is your first time. Once you make a note of your sign for yes, go on to the next calibration question.

Please show me a clear sign for "no." Again, wait for a clear and distinct movement, different from your sign for "yes."

Please show me a clear sign for "need more info." This will be your third and final sign.

For now, all you need to know is when you ask a question and your pendulum shows you the sign for "need more info," it's best for you to revise the question and ask again.

Step 2: Phrase Your Question Mindfully

The quality of the answer you get is directly related to the quality of the question you ask. When you ask, be clear. Here are some suggestions for how to do that, no matter which Truth Testing method you are using.

Start with the phrase "all things considered." I recommend this phrase because it covers all bases, not just what you want, or what your brain thinks, or what your emotions are telling you in the moment. "All things considered" allows you to ask from a Divine perspective, across all time and space, transcending your mind and what is consciously known to you. It is all-encompassing, which means it produces a reliable answer based on a total 360-degree perspective (or perhaps 720 would be more accurate). It's like the difference between asking a question with a mere human brain, and asking a question as the Divine. Sure, the Divine probably wouldn't need to *ask* a question, as it knows all, but let's not tug at that thread just now, mmmkay?

Next, you want to avoid language that implies judgment. Consider that in Divine Mind it's all good. Therefore, you may not get reliable answers if your question contains judgy words like "should," "can," "right/wrong," "good/bad," etc. Instead, stick with the highly effective yet neutral word, "optimal."

When mindfully crafting your question, stick to what you can control right now. Truth Testing is perfect for making decisions and choices, and verifying whether something is true. "Is it optimal for me to call so-and-so?" is a far superior question to "Is so-and-so the right guy for me?" Likewise, "Is it optimal for me to submit my resume to XYZ Company?" is much better than "Is XYZ Company going to hire me?" Focus on what you can do right now, and ask questions that lead you to discover the best choice, decision, or action in this moment.

Lastly, since you are looking for a yes/no answer, stick to just one variable per question. If you could only answer yes or no and someone asked you if you would like five thousand dollars that can be found inside an elephant's ass, you would probably be stumped. Not just because you're wondering where this person has been hanging out lately, but you could not answer if you wanted to say *yes* to five thousand dollars, but *no* to going head-first into an elephant's poop shoot. Whereas if you were asked, "Would you like five thousand dollars?" you could easily answer "yes" and then when asked if you'd like to fish it out of an elephant's rectum, you could (and hopefully, would) politely decline with "no." One variable at a time makes it easier to get a yes/no answer from your pendulum. If you receive a "need more info" sign, it is likely that you sneaked in more than one variable without meaning to do so.

Here are some examples of well-phrased Truth Testing questions:

> All things considered, is it optimal for me to have lunch with Julie?
>
> All things considered, is it optimal for me to book my flight to Jamaica?
>
> All things considered, is this meat optimal to eat? Alternatively, you could ask: all things considered is this meat safe to eat without risk of food poisoning?
>
> All things considered, is Bertha (an employee) stealing from me?

Whereas, these are examples of poorly phrased questions:

> Should I go out with Angela?

Is this the best job for me?

Is Fluffy the poodle going to die?

Is Beverly drunk?

All things considered, does this pendulum make my butt look big?

Step 3: Relax and Await Movement

This is the simplest, yet sometimes the most challenging part of using a pendulum. When you first begin, it may take several minutes before you see movement. It will get faster with practice. Stay focused on the question until the pendulum begins to move. Alternatively, you can distract yourself by clearly phrasing the question, then looking away for a bit. Think of Yoda perhaps. *Patience, young Jedi. Get answer you shall.* Then, when you see movement out of the corner of your eye, remove yourself from the Dagobah swamp and look at the pendulum for your answer.

Anyone can use a pendulum, even children. You can also test another person (or even an animal) by proxy, which can prove very useful in assessments and healing work.

Specifically, to use a pendulum for Truth Testing in the realm of Lightworking, you might consider these applications:

- To verify the truth and accuracy of some information you've just intuited: "All things considered, is it true and accurate that…?"
- To check in and find out whether or not it's optimal to share the information or guidance you just received: "All things considered, is it optimal for me to share this info with ____?"

- To verify whether a particular healing or energy clearing is now complete: "All things considered, is this clearing now complete?" Followed by: "Is there more to clear around this issue?" Followed by: "It is optimal to continue clearing around this issue now?"
- To check in to see whether it's optimal for you to obtain a certain book or training program, or work with a certain Lightworker, or even whether or not it's optimal to take on a particular client: "All things considered, is it optimal for me to (get, work with, etc.) ____?"

Terry: Remember the Magic 8 Ball?

To me, the most helpful thing to build and maintain confidence is to have a truth testing method. There are many methods out there but the most popular are muscle testing, the pendulum, dowsing rods, and oracle cards. I personally use them all. You can search the internet for more info on all of these methods. The pendulum is like an accurate version of the old Magic 8 Ball, remember those? Except of course the pendulum is always correct!

Building self-trust, phasing out self-doubt, and gaining a reliable method for Truth Testing are all steps that will serve you well during this phase. Validation of your abilities helps you learn to fully trust your guides, your intuition, and your inner knowing. This is an exciting part of the process, and the rewards that await you are worthwhile!

The Self-Doubt Checklist and Food for Thought on the next few pages will help you assess your current level of self-doubt and identify ways you can learn to trust yourself more. This will set you up for success once you become ready to move on to the next step in your journey: practicing on other people.

Self-Doubt Checklist

This checklist of questions can help you assess how much self-doubt you currently have.

How do you feel after you make a decision? Do you feel calm and confident/perhaps even hopeful? Or are you second-guessing your choice?

How do you feel before you make a decision? Are you clear and focused, or do you feel scattered and worried?

How do you feel after you get dressed to leave the house for the day? Do you smile at yourself in the mirror, confident and ready to face the day? Or do you worry about how you look?

How do you feel when you're traveling? Are you organized, on time, and relaxed? Or does travel stress you out?

What is your immediate reaction in words, thoughts, and actions when you receive a compliment? Do you take the compliment, or brush it off? ("What, this old thing? I've had it forever. I got it on sale. My cousin was throwing it out, can you believe that? Ugh, please, I'm a mess today.")

How much time do you spend thinking about what other people said/didn't say? The greater the amount, the higher your level of self-doubt.

How long does it take you to make a decision? How long did it take you to answer this question?

Do you feel the need to get input from other people before making a decision? If so, why?

If you find you have a lot of self-doubt, flip back to pages 49-51 and commit to implementing these steps to grow your self-trust. Please don't skip this step—it will make all the difference, and our world needs your Lightworking abilities!

Chapter 4 Food for Thought

1. How do you make decisions currently, and how do you know if something feels true? Do you have a reliable method for truth testing? (If not, we recommend Amy's book *Pendulum Mojo,* available on Amazon.)

2. Trust is a key element of Lightworking. When you receive intuitive guidance or have a form of "knowing," how easily are you able to trust that information? Do you question yourself, the information, or its source (or all three)? What forms of validation have proved helpful for you so far?

3. Take a minute now to review pages 49-51. Which steps will you take today to begin to build and grow your self-trust?

Chapter 5:

Practicing on Others

Since beginning your exploration in Chapter 3, you've likely found at least one Lightworking method you resonate with, and you've begun learning how to practice that method. You may have even worked on yourself a bit. Once you begin to feel comfortable using new methods on yourself, the next step in your journey is to begin practicing on other people.

Oh no, have you fainted a bit? Eyes glazed over? Tempted to skip ahead to the next chapter? It's okay, you're not alone. For some Lightworkers, this is a step that creates massive resistance. Working on ourselves is one thing, but branching out to work on others seems to bring a fresh wave of doubts and fears.

Amy: His Headache Disappeared

Sure, I resisted at first. I remember the first time I cleared for someone else. I was on the phone with a friend of mine who I hadn't known very long. He was an online marketer who wasn't big on spiritual stuff, so I was especially reluctant to mention my newfound skill. But as we talked, he repeatedly complained about a headache, and every time he mentioned it, I got an "intuitive hit" that I could clear it. You can probably imagine what went through my head. What if I can't do it? What if he thinks I'm weird? What if he laughs at me?

*But I finally caved and it **did** work. His headache disappeared! He was amazed and grateful and my perspective began to shift. I realized if I could heal someone else (a skeptic, no less), then certainly there were a lot of people I could help. With more practice, I realized I have a knack for clearing work, so I turned clearing into my profession. Over the years, I have cleared millions of limiting beliefs for thousands of individuals, subsequently empowering them to become far more successful in life, in love, and in business.*

Working on Strangers vs. People You Know

For most Lightworkers, the choice to begin practicing on total strangers feels counterintuitive. Our tendency is to stay inside our safety zone and start practicing on people we know. After all, we know them, right? We know their issues, their skepticisms, their strengths and weaknesses. Besides, these people love us, so of course it seems natural to think they would be the most open and receptive to what we're offering. Right? Wrong!

In most cases, it's far easier to practice on a total stranger than on someone you know. Here are some reasons why:

- You have less bias when working with strangers, because you have no history with them.
- There's less interference from your brain, since you don't know anything about this person. This is helpful so you can relax and just let intuitive guidance flow.

- Your family and friends have a certain filter through which they see you. Your history together can prevent them from hearing you as an expert, especially if you're just starting out. Even more so if it's your older sister who still remembers when you were in diapers.
- It's easier to deliver truth to a perfect stranger than to someone you are already closely connected to…especially if that truth is not particularly good news.
- Strangers are often more open-minded because they don't know you personally and they view you as an objective expert in your field.
- In many cases, strangers are more likely to provide you with honest feedback during and after the session, as opposed to someone close to you.
- People you know may act as though it's all right for you to practice on them, and they may even give you verbal permission to do so. But inside, they may still feel resistant, skeptical, or worried that you'll learn some of their secrets they're not quite ready to reveal. Their resistance and underlying reluctance can result in a less than stellar session that leaves you feeling inadequate or confused.
- Strangers are coming to you for your professional help; friends sometimes think they're doing YOU a favor by letting you practice on them! Can you see how this distinction would shift the energy of the session?

A Word About Permission

Different Lightworkers have different opinions about *permission*. Some believe it's always best to obtain verbal permission before working on anyone, and some professional Lightworkers begin every session by obtaining this permission. Some Lightworkers who perform bodywork require their clients sign a formal waiver, granting written permission and outlining any potential risks. Other Lightworkers assume they have permission under certain parameters. For example, if a client hires Amy for healing work, she automatically interprets this as permission and begins the work. The same is true if a friend or family member asks her for intuitive help or healing. But if Amy's client asks her to check in for another person (the client's spouse, friend, etc.), that's when Amy would check (energetically) with that person's Highest Self to see if they are okay with proceeding in this way.

As you begin to practice on other people, you will be able to feel into which approach feels best to you. Any strong feelings that you experience around permission are worth exploring, as they are likely related to your own issues, and not the person you're practicing on. For example, if you feel as though asking permission is a hassle or a frustration, there's likely some underlying block you're holding that's prompting such feelings. On the other hand, if you feel anxious or nervous unless you get written or verbal permission, this is likely related to underlying fear you're carrying.

Avoid using your desire to help as a justification to "barge into" another person's energy or give unwanted guidance. The more you practice, and the more receptive you are to sensing shifts in subtle energy, the more aware you will become of when others are open or not to receiving assistance and guidance from you. If you receive intuitive information for someone, but you're not certain whether or not they are open to receiving it, you can always use Truth Testing to check in: All things considered, is it optimal for me to share this now? If the answer is no, or if the person is clearly not receptive, then please respect that.

Lady Roxanna: Don't Tell Me, I Don't Wanna Know

I have found that it is easier to read for strangers than family, because with strangers, I don't question any information that comes through. If you know the person well, you tend to filter information by thinking, "Is this just because I know them so well, or is it truly the message?" I find this really comes into play when I'm doing mediumship readings. The less I know about the client, the easier the information flows. Of course, sometimes they don't recognize the spirit you are talking about, so they may have some doubt or even resistance on their side, either not believing it, or saying "that's not for me."

Once I did a reading for a girl I had literally just met. I gave her tons of information, of which she understood a little, but couldn't really confirm because the spirit was two generations back in her family. As I told her, "It's a great aunt, she's telling me the name Jenny," she remembered that her mom was called Jenny as a child. I advised her to check with her mother's side of the family and research this information, which seemed to ease her mind.

*Even though I **can** do healing on my family members, I don't tend to do readings for them. Because we are so close, reading their energy feels chaotic to me. When we were younger, I used to tell my husband things all the time, until one day he told me, "Don't tell me, I don't wanna know." So, to respect his free will, I stopped telling him things I knew. My son is now a teenager (which has a totally different feel of chaos) so I stay out energetically unless he asks me for Reiki.*

Group work is another interesting aspect of practicing on other people. The upside is that it provides immediate feedback, as other members of the group can immediately validate the information you're receiving. This is especially helpful if the person you're receiving for is resistant about hearing the information. Also, in many group settings, the work tends to bounce around the circle. For example, someone else might have the first piece of information, and then you might have the next, and yet another person may have the actual healing or clearing. It also gives you the opportunity to learn by observing other Lightworkers as they give and receive throughout the group session.

Jen: Group Work Has Many Benefits

My first experience working with others occurred at group retreats. It was extremely helpful to have the immediate feedback that allowed me to know if what I was getting was in harmony with what the group was getting. It allowed to me to turn off ego/intellect/autopilot and simply allow information to flow through me. Plus, in a group setting I was able to notice the impact of judging information as weird, too harsh, or unlikely. I could see how any of these slowed down the flow of information and the progress of the group. Often, I would be on track with the group, in the flow, and then if I stopped to question something in my mind, the group would continue moving forward and gather more information about a topic while I pondered. Those workshops were a great segue for me to step into paid client work. The safety net of the group helped me to verify when I was operating from ego vs. when I was allowing information from higher consciousness to flow through. This was a powerful change for me because up until that point, I had only been using a pendulum or muscle testing, which had felt forced and like guesswork.

Terry: I LOVE Retreats!

I highly recommend that you make it a point to get to as many retreats as you can—at least once if not twice a year. They are such invaluable and incredible tools for mind, body, and spirit. Retreats have many benefits like personal growth, bonding with likeminded people, healing, and oh yeah—clearing! I have attended quite a few retreats and all of them have proven to be very beneficial in my mental, emotional, and spiritual growth. Group work is so very rewarding, and I always leave a retreat on a natural high.

Amy: There's No Right Way

I remember attending a retreat where a newly exploring Lightworker actually discovered her ability right in front of us! She had a sibling who had died, and we all felt that this sibling had a message to pass through to the group, but it would only come through her sister. After being still and open for many minutes with no messages coming through, she abruptly stood up and left the room. She returned a minute later and apologized, as she had gone to retrieve her laptop from her bag. She said she felt embarrassed because this was a spiritual retreat, and here she was, picking up her laptop, of all things! She then sat down, opened the clamshell, and closed her eyes. Almost immediately, she began to type. She had no idea what she had written until she opened her eyes and read the message out loud to us. It was evident it had come from her sister. She continued to receive messages in this way throughout the rest of the retreat (and for all I know, she still does this today). I was awestruck! It had never occurred to me that information could come through in such a unique and personal way. This is when I began to realize that each Lightworker is truly one of a kind, and there are no "right ways" to do this important work.

How to Know if You're Improving

As we become more mindful on our path as a Lightworker, we can notice how our relationships, interactions, and circumstances begin to change as we ourselves change. These observations can be very useful, as we can look around ourselves to find evidence of our growth.

Here are a few of the indicators that can show signs of your improvement:

- The speed with which intuitive information begins to flow and/or healings occur.

- The quality of intuitive information that you receive.
- The efficiency of your work on yourself and others.
- The accuracy of the information you receive and share.
- The efficacy of the healing work you perform.
- The depth and breadth of information you are able to intuit.
- The lessening of doubt about yourself, your abilities, and the intuitive information you receive.
- The amount of fun you have while working on yourself or others.

It is important to mention that when it comes to improvement, ensure you only measure where *you were* to where *you are* today. Resist the urge to compare yourself to others, which only leads to compare and despair. Consider that the best, most innovative chefs are constantly working to expand their own palate and push their own skills and abilities beyond their own limits. They are not chasing after other great chefs; rather, they are stretching their own limits and competing against themselves.

Jen: It Felt Gray and Unstable

After I had attended a few retreats and worked in groups, I enrolled in a health coaching program, completed the coursework and began working towards certification. The first clients that I worked with were energetically needy, very low paying, and were not fun to work with. Even though I was paid, these first clients felt more like practice clients in a lot of ways. I received very little money for the work (about $35 an hour), I didn't have my coaching session procedure clearly defined, and I wasn't sure what my niche was.

When I think back on how I felt about my career, it felt gray and unstable. I felt I needed to justify what I was doing to my friends and family, I was unsure of myself, and I was afraid to overcharge people because I wasn't sure how valid what I was doing really was. The clients I attracted reflected all of these beliefs that I held about myself and my work at that time.

It's important to your own growth and development that you remember to acknowledge your progress and celebrate your wins. This is yet another way to develop self-trust and eradicate self-doubt. When you notice any form of improvement—as a Lightworker or simply as a person—take time to honor and appreciate your own success. You might treat yourself to something special like a massage or flowers, or you may simply choose to smile and marvel at how far you've come.

Amy: You Can't Reason with an Unreasonable Person

*It's fascinating to me how much our outer world reflects our inner world. I see the greatest evidence of growth when I notice my feelings and reactions toward certain things, people, and situations. In the past, if someone had been rude to me, or tried to accuse me of something that wasn't true, I'd get completely spun out. I'm talking, **for days** at a time. I would replay conversations over and over again in my mind, wishing I had said something wittier, or stuck up for myself more, or told off the other person. Today, I don't rattle as easily. I'm much more inclined to speak my truth, and I've learned you can't reason with an unreasonable person.*

If someone tells me, "You made me feel this way," I now understand how untrue that is, because I can't make anyone feel anything. We are each responsible for our own feelings. I can choose to calmly say, "That's not what happened," or I can choose not to engage. Either way, it's interesting to observe. If I know I'm not a bitch, but someone is certain I am, why would I waste my time and energy trying to convince them otherwise? Instead I think, "Hmmm, you think I'm a bitch, fascinating! I wonder what's going on in your life that would cause you to think that?"

Sure, I'm still human, and my feelings get hurt from time to time, but no way do I waste days or even hours thinking about it. Today I can notice it, process my feelings, do a quick clearing or cord cutting if I need to, and move on. It's extraordinary how liberating that single transformation has been.

Recognizing Resistance

Once you branch out and start practicing on other people, it will become increasingly important for you to learn to recognize resistance in other people. This is challenging in the beginning, before you've laid the groundwork for solid self-trust, and before you fully trust your guides. You could be working on someone, or delivering intuitive messages to them, and if they disagree or don't validate your message, you may be inclined to second-guess yourself (as we explored in depth in the previous chapter).

In many cases, whatever information you received was accurate, but the other person simply may not have been ready to receive that information. This is what we refer to as "resistance." Resistance is simply a refusal to accept. For example, you may have felt resistance when you first realized that you were a Lightworker. You may not have wanted to accept that as truth, and so you resisted your calling.

The key in recognizing resistance is to do so **without judgment.** There's nothing inherently wrong with a person not being ready to accept a certain truth. Do not view this as a fault of that person's, but rather, an area in which they need some assistance in moving through. If you were resistant at first to accepting your role as a Lightworker, that's fine, right? It is neither good nor bad, it just simply is. Because here you are today, nearly halfway through *The Lightworker's Guide to Getting Started.* This work isn't about who gets there the fastest; rather, it is all about the journey itself.

Lightworkers have a wonderful saying that works on many levels:

It is what it is.

"It is what it is" is a simple truth that helps us to accept what's already so. Acceptance doesn't mean we're stuck with our current situation or problem forever; it simply means we accept the truth right now, in this moment. This is an integral key to transformation.

Jen: She Hung up on Me

One of my earliest clients would hang up the phone on me when we touched on patterns of behavior that she didn't want to examine. Talk about resistance! Often when challenging topics arise while working with clients over the phone, there is a technical difficulty. The call or video chat will drop, or we'll hear static or crackling on the line. Sometimes the information I'm presenting doesn't land. I'll say it a few different ways, and the client just cannot hear it.

When this happens, I ask the guides for a smaller step or perhaps a way to come at the knot from another direction, so the release is more accessible for the client. Whether or not this is effective depends on the willingness of the client. I prefer not to press clients to the point of defensiveness, if possible. I can usually feel tightening in my abdomen if the client is getting tense or the topic is too challenging, and that signals me to find a different way to come at the release work more gently.

Sometimes, all a person needs to release their resistance is time. They may need the choice to feel like their own, or they may need to process some feelings around a difficult truth. Other times, coaching with a firm yet compassionate approach is the solution. And yet, there are times when some individuals never become ready to accept the truth.

Amy: A Worst Case Scenario

For years, I used an anonymous platform as a way for me to give back and to practice new healing methods. One day, a man asked me to clear something for him. He was hearing voices in his head, telling him that he was attracted to other men. He found this especially disturbing, not only because the man was convinced he was straight, but also because the voice in his head seemed very judgmental. The voice called him names and made derogatory comments about his sexuality. This upset him greatly, and so he asked me to clear it for him.

I checked in objectively, because that's what I always do and besides, what difference does it make to me if this man is gay or not gay? I had no bias, I only wanted to help him. When I checked in intuitively, it became very clear that the man is in fact gay. I knew this information would not be well-received by the man, so I had two other intuitives verify that my information was correct (while maintaining the man's privacy, of course). "Oh dear," I thought. I tapped into kindness and compassion as I drafted a carefully worded response, inviting the man to practice self-acceptance and live into this new truth. I felt certain that in time, he would free himself with this new truth.

Wow, talk about your worst case scenario of resistance! Not only was he furious with me, but he started sending me hateful messages and accusing me of working witchcraft on his mind because, can you guess? The voices telling him he was gay had grown louder and more persistent. Whatever we resist persists, and this man was a living example of that. Inner conflict is often the harshest conflict of all.

People...People Who Need (Practice) People...

Where can you find strangers who are willing to let you practice on them? Sure, you might like to know the name of the anonymous platform Amy was using so you can stay away from it, but keep in mind resistance can show up anywhere, so don't let that scare you away! We don't often hear stories like Amy's from newbie Lightworkers. This level of intense resistance is something that normally shows up later in a Lightworker's learning curve, as a way of helping push us to grow even more. Amy was a well-established healer when she encountered the massive resistance from this man, and as a result, she grew as a person and as a Lightworker.

Here are a few ways you can find people to practice on:

- Join some social media groups, such as Facebook groups. Many people here are willing to receive free healing work in exchange for providing you with honest feedback. Nowadays you can find a Facebook group for most any type of Lightworker or healing modality.
- For starters, join our Lightworker's Guide to Getting Started private community. Here you're sure to meet some folks who are at exactly the same point where you now find yourself! Plus, they're just cool people because that's who we the authors tend to attract.

TheLightworkersGuide.com

- Check out your local metaphysical shop. Most sizable cities have at least one, or it may be worth a day trip to travel to a nearby town. Try searching stores under "new age," "crystals," or "spiritual shop." Many shops have a bulletin board where local Lightworkers can post flyers and business cards, and some shops host classes, workshops, and small gatherings. If you're in the Connecticut area, connect with Jen, she's got a healing center of her own there.
- Take classes. From yoga to tarot readings to

mediumship, local classes help you to build your network while you learn. Some classes and programs (such as Reiki) have you practice on fellow students while you are learning.

- Be smart and be safe. Don't post on Craigslist or flyer your neighborhood. Start by connecting with like-minded Lightworkers and make your practice requests from there. Don't be afraid to ask someone much more experienced than you if you can practice on them. You might be thinking, "Why would they want *me* to work on them?" but you just never know. They may not know anyone else who shares your modality, or they might need the help right now (you could be the answer to their prayers), or they simply like you. Besides which, experienced people tend to know a lot of people. Even if they decline, odds are they know someone else they could refer to you.

Terry: Social Media Is My Jam

I have discovered through social media that Lightworkers now have many forums in which to learn, grow, and practice. I strongly suggest finding some groups of like-minded people to practice on but also to learn from and grow with. This is a very inexpensive option, but there are some things to watch out for. You may be learning from people with less experience than you have, or you may attract people who only want to sell you on their own programs and healing services. You might also find yourself among "takers," which makes it very important for you to set boundaries.

For some people, it is easier and better to practice in groups and for others, one-on-one is best. If you prefer one-on-one learning, it is optimal to seek out an experienced coach/mentor with whom you bond; one you are drawn to and feel at ease with. This learning style can be accomplished long distance or face-to-face. I strongly feel it is of great value for everyone to have a mentor throughout their journey. Being a Lightworker is definitely not a one-man or one-woman show, so why would learning be?

A Few Caveats to Consider

There are a few caveats to working on other people. For starters, you're likely to experience some discomfort whenever you have to deliver bad news. In most cases, this is a sign of your resistance, and has nothing to do with the other person. More about that in the next chapter.

Another caveat involves unexpected (or unwanted) entanglement. For example, what if your BFF asks you to check in intuitively to find out whether or not her husband is cheating on her? Yikes, that is one sticky situation. What if a total stranger asks you to check in as to whether or not the lump in their neck is cancerous? What if the person for whom you did a free reading now calls and texts you constantly, asking you to check in on other stuff for them? For free, of course.

This is where boundaries become essential. We will talk more about protecting your energy in an upcoming chapter, but for now, consider how boundaries could prevent unpleasant situations like the ones described in the above paragraph. Here's the rub: **Lightworkers are inherently helpers.** We don't like telling people "no" because we want to be of service and we really just want to help. Which means, generally speaking, we suck at setting boundaries. We suck so badly at it!

Most Lightworkers have had to condition themselves over time to set and maintain boundaries. We'd like to help you get a head start on this, so begin by saying these practice statements out loud:

- No, I wouldn't feel comfortable doing that.

- Let's see if we can find someone else who can help you with that.
- That's outside my area of expertise. Here's what I can help you with instead:
- I'm not a medical professional. Is there something else I can check for you today?
- Let's stay on topic here.
- Let's put a pin in that for now.
- I'm not guided to do that.
- That doesn't feel optimal right now.

Setting and holding boundaries are a byproduct of self-love and self-trust. As you progress, these boundaries may shift, but it's good to have something in place from the get-go. Your work from the previous chapter, and the Food for Thought questions at the end of this chapter can help you to set appropriate "starter" boundaries as you begin practicing on other people. Remember, you always have the right to say no.

By the same token, we can respect the boundaries of others by giving them enough space when they are not receptive to whatever guidance or healing we may have for them. If they're not ready or willing to hear what we know, that is their choice, and that is fine. If you then find yourself feeling frustrated or judgmental by their stance, understand that those feelings are *yours,* not theirs. Fortunately, we are always free to work on our own issues!

Chapter 5 Food for Thought...and a Tasting!

Before practicing on others, it is always a good idea to take care of yourself first. Let's clear the mind and get present in the here and now. Please take a few minutes now to do this exercise now:

- Sit quietly with your eyes closed.
- Scan your body from your head to your toes, as you note and release any and all tension.
- Place your feet flat on the ground, preferably barefoot.
- Take several slow and deep breaths, inhaling through your nose and exhaling out through your pursed lips, as if you were blowing out a candle.
- Empty your mind completely, for as long as you can.
- Be aware of the thoughts that do break through, acknowledge and remove each one.
- Focus on gratitude and bliss as you continue to breathe.
- Open your eyes.

1. Were you able to empty your mind for more than a minute before unwelcomed thoughts floated in? What kind of thoughts crossed your mind? Were they random, or thoughts of boredom or disbelief? How did you feel (cold, hot, happy, sad, etc.)?

2. Did you see anything in your mind's eye, such as pictures, videos, or colors? Did you hear anything like music, a high pitch tone, or a voice with your external or even internal (spiritual) ears? Did you smell any scents like perfume, flowers, or something pungent, or taste any flavors like bitter, sweet, metallic, or salty? Write about your experience with this activity. Now apply the same when practicing on plants, animals, people, etc., and see what comes up.

3. Here is a wonderful exercise to help you obtain confidence in setting boundaries. Using the practice statements below, stand in front of a mirror and look at yourself as though you are your future successful self, talking to you in this moment. Say each statement with conviction. Repeat this process until any adverse feelings have dissipated, and you can say each statement with calm confidence.

- No, I wouldn't feel comfortable doing that.
- Let's see if we can find someone else who can help you with that.
- That's outside my area of expertise. Here's what I can help you with instead:
- I'm not a medical professional. Is there something else I can check for you today?
- Let's stay on topic here.
- Let's put a pin in that for now.

Chapter 6:

The Filtering Caveat

As human beings, we perceive life around us (and even ourselves) through various filters. It's like a screen that lets what we perceive pass through our understandings of the world. Part of the challenge of being a Lightworker involves learning to release our filters so that we can access Truth and best fulfill our calling.

It might surprise you to learn that many Lightworkers of today grew up in very religious households. Can you imagine how the filters of certain organized religions would impact today's Lightworker? So that we don't pick on any one religion, let's invent an imaginary rule.

Let's say for the sake of this example that Lucy Lightworker held onto some very strong religious beliefs which said it is a sin to drive a car. Essentially, cars are the antichrist in this religion, and anyone who owns, drives, or rides in a car will surely burn in Spaltry (that's what this religions calls "Hell." Hey, as long as we're making things up, might as well have fun with it, right?) Every day, Lucy and her fellow religious community members pray for each other's souls so that they can each be saved from Spaltry.

One day, Lucy signs a new Lightworking client, but ten minutes into their first session, the client reveals that she is an Uber driver. How do you think this might impact Lucy's perception of the client? Would Lucy be able to hold a loving space of acceptance for the session? What are the odds that Lucy would be able to remain objective as her new client shares her concerns and frustrations (and perhaps low back pain) about driving customers around all day?

Lucy's filter would most likely prevent her from being open and receptive in working with a client whose occupation was in direct opposition to Lucy's religious beliefs.

To be clear, we're not saying that Lightworkers can't be religious, or that a religious Lightworker can't be good at what they do. That's not necessarily the case. In Lucy's (imaginary) situation, she might find it prudent to only work with members of her own religion, or the Amish, or children under the driving age. Alternatively, she might have prospective clients fill out a pre-enrollment questionnaire, during which she could ask them whether they are pro- or anti-auto.

We're also not saying Lightworkers should only work with people who share their beliefs. That's not true, especially given that some Lightworkers are here specifically to expand minds and help individuals open up to new beliefs and possibilities.

Rather, we're taking this time to demonstrate how *filters* affect our perceptions. Because the more you understand this concept, the easier it will be to recognize your own filters as you're working with people as a Lightworker. You will also be able to recognize when the person you're working with is filtering the message you're sharing with them, which may wind up diluting its truth and validity.

We are human. Therefore, we naturally perceive our world through the filters we have created through experience, belief, and understanding. This is normal and is not an issue. The caveat is this: when working as a Lightworker, it is vital to deliver the message *as you receive it*. If you let your brain process intuitive guidance through your filters, rather than sharing the unadulterated message, you are not serving the very person you are working with.

What? (You ask.) Why would we alter a message so pure and special as to have been delivered from the Divine? Excellent question. When we first start out as Lightworkers, we tend to alter and modify intuitive messages for many reasons, such as:

- fear
- discomfort
- our own resistance
- our own issues that we don't want to face
- our own beliefs and positions and bias
- our perceived/anticipated resistance from the other person
- we don't want to deliver bad news
- we may have a blocked throat chakra
- we worry they'll shoot the messenger
- we don't want to look stupid/weird/wrong/incompetent
- we don't like conflict and confrontation
- we don't want them to be mad at us
- the message makes no sense to our logical brain
- we don't understand the message
- other reasons we don't understand at the time

Do you see a pattern in the above list? Perhaps you noticed that nearly everything on the list has to do with us, the messenger! We'd like to invite you to consider that *whenever* you have resistance to delivering an intuitive message exactly as you receive it, it likely has everything to do with you and nothing to do with the other person.

Amy: Watch out for that Lion

While I was still a Lightworking newbie, I received some disturbing news to deliver at a group retreat. I witnessed the gruesome scene in my mind, unfolding plain as day, and it was horrifying. In this past life vision, a member of our group found herself face to face with a lion, decided to run, and the lion pounced on her from behind. In my mind's eye, I watched the lion rake its claws down this woman's back, knocking her to the ground. It then devoured her flesh. I was mortified, nauseated, and highly resistant to relaying this message. It took me forever to spit it out. I described in great detail the meadow, the weather, and the psychology of a fight or flight response. The woman hung on my every word, waiting for me to get to the good stuff. The group leader gently prompted me to get on with it already.

I used many disclaimers and apologies as I slowly described what I saw. I felt terrible to have to tell her all of this, and yet for the woman, light bulbs were going off like crazy. "Ah!" she exclaimed. "So that's why I get chills up and down my back whenever I have to make a decision!" She was eating it up, no pun intended. Why then did I feel so awful? It was only later in the retreat that I realized why I had been so resistant to deliver the message to her. Because in that past lifetime, I was the damn lion!

That's right, we filter because of **our own stuff,** not because of theirs, or because of the message itself. The Ego can start a-chatterin' in our minds whenever an intuitive message comes through that's not all sparkles and rainbows. "Oooh, don't say that," it chides us. "He is not gonna wanna hear that." "You can't say that, how could you possibly know that?" "Well, that's just rude. Let's say basically the same thing, but in a much nicer way."

Jen: Taboo Topics

At the very beginning, I worked with several women who were either going through peri-menopause or were post-menopausal. I felt a lot of discomfort talking about their sex lives, body sensations, and barriers to being intimate with their partners. Ultimately I was able to relax and the information that came through was very helpful, but it took a while in each of those sessions for me to relax enough in order to just be open and listen.

Amy: I've Heard Things I Can't Un-Hear

For two years, I did regular coaching and healing work over the phone for a client who worked in the sex trade. Boy, did that push my edges! She and I could not have been more different at that time. She spoke unabashedly about everything related to sex, and I often wondered if she could sense my energy as I wanted to crawl under my desk and hide. I remember feeling grateful our sessions were over the phone, so she could never see me blushing!

Working with this individual pushed me to have to work on my own issues and inhibitions around sex, which wasn't something I was expecting or prepared for. I also found I had to work on a lot of judgments I had around individuals who exhibit freedom in their sex and sexuality. I knew I could not be a good coach and help this person if I was silently and secretly judging her. The whole experience really forced me to grow as a coach, as a healer, and as a person. Thanks to her, I was able to access a deeper level of compassion and acceptance for my fellow humans.

Today, there is literally nothing a client can say in a session that will shock me or cause me to judge them. I am certain I could not have achieved this level of neutrality and suspension of Ego, had I not worked with this particular client so many years ago. So often our greatest challenges in Lightworking ultimately turn out to be our biggest blessings.

Speaking with Disclaimers

As mentioned in a prior chapter, until you have a well-developed foundation of trust with yourself and your guides, you may find yourself speaking in disclaimers. When we talk about disclaimers in this context, we are referring to the need to preface your messages with an escape clause. As you progress on your Lightworker journey, you can drop these disclaimers as they are no longer necessary, plus they tend to diminish the intuitive messages you're delivering. Some individuals who aren't Lightworkers speak in disclaimers frequently due to low self-esteem.

See if any of these sound familiar:

> "I know this may sound crazy but..."
> "This doesn't make sense to me but it may to you..."
> "I don't know if any of this is true but this is what I am getting."
> "This may sound totally out of left field but..."
> "This is probably gonna sound weird but..."
> "I know this sounds (may sound) crazy, but here's what I'm getting..."
> "I don't really get this, but here's what I'm getting..."
> "Nothing is set in stone, but in this moment, I'm getting..."
> "I'm sorry to tell you this, but..."

"OK, keep in mind, I'm just the messenger, but..."
"...but the moment you walk out the door the decision you make to turn right or left could change your path."
"You can decide if this feels true for you..."
"I don't want to be the one to tell you this, but..."
"Do you know anything about...?"

Lady Roxanna: Sometimes Disclaimers Happen

I have used many disclaimers in the past, but not so much anymore, unless the information doesn't make sense to me and I can't figure it out. In that case, I might be inclined to relay that to them, to see if we can figure it out together. I find these to be true when channeling for people because they don't always recognize the spirit right away, or the messages they are using to identify themselves to their loved one. I do always try to convey information exactly as I receive it, without filtering.

The Authors: Then and Now

In the beginning, if we got guidance that didn't resonate (for example, something went wrong; the person didn't validate the info; or the person disagreed with the intuitive message; etc.), we would feel stupid and pissed off and not supported by Spirit. We would feel scared, unsupported, and apprehensive to continue. We would be unable to finish without Ego getting in the way. We would question the reality of it all and think we must be crazy. Now if that happens, we just relax and roll with it. If we're uncertain, we use truth testing to verify. But we know the information we receive is accurate, and that not everyone is ready to receive the messages we are given to share with them.

The purpose of this book is to help you avoid repeating our mistakes. Hopefully, by now you can see that almost everything "weird" you're experiencing is actually considered "normal" for Lightworkers. It is safe for you to trust your inner knowing. You can relax and know that your guides have got your back. The sooner you learn to share the messages and guidance you receive, the smoother your journey will become.

Amy: What Did I Just Say?

I'm so in the moment when I'm receiving information for someone that I often can't recall what I just said. I can't tell you how many times a client has said, "Can you repeat that?" and yet I have no access to whatever's just come out of my mouth. "No, but I can receive it again," I say, and that's what I do.

Here are a few tips to help you to share exactly the messages you receive, without filtering, analyzing, modifying, or using disclaimers:

1. **Post a reminder** in your space or review a reminder before you begin a session. It can be a simple as "Just spit it out," or "Trust your inner knowing," or even, "We've got this."

2. Just before you begin a session, **ask your Ego to go out for coffee** for a bit, and to take your filters with it. Amy calls this method "Ego in a Box" and many of Amy's clients have found this simple technique to be quite helpful with a noisy and intrusive Ego.

3. When you hear yourself speaking a disclaimer, or starting to modify a message, immediately **stop and say "cancel"** or draw an "x" in the air with your finger. Take a deep breath and begin again. If you've then forgotten the message, ask for it to come to you again.

4. **Use a notebook.** You can write down a message exactly as you're receiving it, then take a minute to release your inhibitions about sharing the message exactly. This is helpful for introverts who need a minute or so to process

information before speaking.

5. **Give yourself permission to take your time.** Often we hate for others to wait for us, so we rush through important parts of sessions in order to avoid awkward silences. But remember, you can always lay out ground rules before you work with someone, or at the beginning of a session. Something to the effect of this works wonders to put you both at ease: "As we're working together, you may hear long pauses. This is normal and happens when I'm receiving intuitive guidance for you."

Jen: I Now Know Not to Get Flustered

Early on, if the information I got didn't make sense for the client and there was no obvious connection to the work at hand, I would freeze up and get derailed. I'd start trying to find a logical connection or a way to work the guidance logically into what we were working through, which felt like forcing a puzzle piece into place. I might have felt a little flush as my cheeks turned red, and I would have shut off the flow of information at that point. It would have taken me a bit to calm down, get re-centered and reconnect to higher guidance. Sometimes the information would make sense by the end of the session, once more information came through. Sometimes I would make the connection later while driving and email the client with the insight. Once the pressure of being in the session was over and I could completely relax, more information was available to me.

Now, if that happens, I know not to get flustered. I just skip it and move to the next piece of information. I notice I'm not judging the process nearly as much as I used to. If I feel like we reach a temporary dead end, I move on and stay in the flow. I remind myself that the guidance is always correct and to just speak whatever information I receive.

Remember to be gentle with yourself during this process. Becoming a Lightworker takes practice and patience, so be sure to give yourself the space to learn as you go, to occasionally stumble, but also to soar. These Food for Thought questions will help.

Chapter 6 Food for Thought

1. Have you had any religious experience? In what ways have you benefitted from this? In what ways has it been detrimental to your growth? Do you have residual feelings of fear, guilt, or doubt as a result? Are there beliefs within the religion(s) that you don't agree with or that limit your potential? How do you think your answers impact your ability to be a Lightworker?

2. Think of at least five Lightworkers you are familiar with and notice how they speak without using disclaimers. For example, Sylvia Brown speaks in a confident, matter-of-fact manner. Hollywood Medium Tyler Henry scribbles on paper as he lays out information.

3. Say the following out loud, and notice how you feel: "I KNOW WHAT I KNOW." You may wish to use this mantra several times with passion and meaning before practicing on others.

Chapter 7:

Clearing Your Crap

Expanding Your Own Channel

The best Lightworkers we (the authors) know are all still working on themselves, releasing their own blocks and limitations, expanding their awareness, and continuing to grow as individuals. Beware the Lightworker who feels he or she has "arrived" and thinks the work on himself or herself is finished! We understand that the better we become, the better we can serve others.

Any time we are faced with unpleasantness, whether in the line of Lightworking or simply in life in general, there is an opportunity for growth. For many Lightworkers, we rely upon healing and clearing methods to help release our own fears, emotional upsets, and limitations as we become aware of them. Some issues may feel a bit intense, heavy, or huge for us to handle on our own, and this is why many Lightworkers choose to have our own coaches, healers, and experts.

Amy: Never on My Own

I've always been strong-willed, independent, and self-reliant. As a Lightworker, I endured most of my personal journey alone, and I've cleared millions of blocks for tens of thousands of individuals. But guess what? If one of my own children gets sick or injured, my intuition is no good to them. In these situations, I must rely on other healers and Lightworkers to check in objectively for me and many times, to complete any necessary healing work for my kids. Do you know how hard it is for a self-reliant person to have to ask for help? What a blessing this lesson has been for me! I have learned to rely on other healers, coaches, and experts and my journey has been immensely enriched by them.

In fact, the healers I rely on most are those who began as my clients, then we evolved into friends and colleagues, and now they are trusted resources and cherished loved ones. As much as I appreciate my time alone to write, to reflect, and to recharge, I am so very grateful to have so many wonderful and gifted Lightworkers in my life. Because of this I know I will never be "on my own" again, and that's a good thing.

Keeping Your Energy Clean

The work of a Lightworker is rewarding and exquisite and delightful; but it is not without consequence. As you begin to work on other people, it becomes essential that you keep your own energy clean. This not only benefits the work you do, but also your own personal well-being. Self-trust is connected to self-love, remember? Lightworkers continue to work on self-love, and the deeper we dive into this, the better everything in life becomes. The more we are able to love and value ourselves, the easier it becomes to practice self-care. Think back to Chapter 5 where we talked about the importance of setting and keeping boundaries as one aspect of self-care. Another aspect of self-love and self-care involves keeping your energy clean.

Have you ever seen the cooking show *The Worst Cooks in America*? Anne Burrell goes head to head with another chef (from Rachael Ray to Bobby Flay) and in just a few short weeks, they each attempt to teach the country's worst cooks how to prepare a gourmet meal. The final challenge involves a blind tasting by a panel of culinary experts and the winner (Chef Anne or her opponent) is the one whose student was able to wow the judges. It's a fun show to watch because it's all about rapid transformation. The shift is remarkable because each of these individuals starts the season knowing *nothing* about cooking. One contestant actually asked, "Is this a stove, or an oven?" But by the end of the show, everyone's crying and thanking their chef coach as they talk about how they are so grateful they can now eat healthy at home, save money, and share love by cooking food for their own children, their spouse, their friends, or anyone else. An area of their life where they felt weak or inadequate has completely shifted to the point of empowerment and excitement. Like Lightworking, it's never just about the food (or the work)—it's about the *transformation*.

In this show (and probably in real life), Chef Anne Burrell yells...*a lot*. One of her biggest pet peeves is a messy work station. She's constantly hollering at her cooking recruits to clean up after themselves, work neat, get rid of their mess, etc.

If you've ever taken any cooking classes or learned how to cook like a pro, this is a lesson you understand. An inexperienced home cook or a new cook is disorganized, easily flustered, and by the time the food is ready, the kitchen looks like a bomb went off. An experienced cook with expert training cleans as they go and keeps their workspace neat and tidy. Not only does this serve practical purposes (avoiding cross-contamination, facilitating faster cleanup, etc.), but it also puts the cook in a calmer state of mind, allowing them to remain grounded and in control while cooking. A chaotic workspace leads to a chaotic mindset. Besides, after you finally sit down to enjoy the meal you've worked so hard to prepare, the last thing you want to do after that is face a trashed kitchen!

Whether you cook or not, and whether you tend to work neatly or not in the kitchen, can you see the value of keeping order and cleanliness? Good, because this is key in energy work. So much energy moves in every session, and so much gunk is extracted and dissipated and shifted! If you don't keep your workspace clean and clear, and keep your own energy field clean and clear, you're going to feel chaotic during the session and then drained and exhausted afterwards.

Amy: Spiritual Detox

*The single best thing any Lightworker can do to take care of herself is to drink more water. Not coffee, not tea, not kombucha, or flavored waters, but just plain water. Maybe with a twist of lemon, if you really can't stand the taste of water. You must always remember, no matter how it may appears on the surface, you are a vessel through which healing flows. You are moving tons of energy in every session, in every encounter with other human beings. If you don't take care of your body, it will break down. It is your job to be a good steward of your body, and this begins with the most fundamental element on our planet: **water.** I advise all my clients to double up on their water intake for twenty-four to forty-eight hours after a session. I drink vast amounts of water because I'm also participating in their big energy shifts.*

If after a session, you feel tired, drained, sleepy, or if you have a headache or feel nauseous, that is almost always an indication that you're not consuming enough water. Each energy clearing is like a spiritual detox, and because we are walking around in bodies while we do this, our bodies need to be able to release and process as well. Water is the greatest facilitator to do this.

And then there's chocolate. Whenever I'm writing, I always have some high quality dark chocolate on hand. Writing for me is similar to channeling, and chocolate helps me to stay grounded and focused while I've got this massive crown chakra connection open and flowing. Yes, if you're a Lightworker who writes, I'm officially prescribing chocolate for your well-being.

Pick Your (Un)Poison

There are many ways to keep your energy clean before, during, and after you engage in Lightworking duties. Here are just a few examples of our favorites.

- drinking lots of water
- setting a sacred space in which to work
- grounding. We recommend Amy's book *Get Grounded* (available on Amazon).
- smudging with a sage stick (available at most metaphysical shops)
- meditation
- eat a tiny amount of high quality salt and/or a small piece of dark chocolate
- Reiki
- placing healing items in your space: Himalayan salt lamps, crystals, water fountains, plants, art that you love or have made, etc.
- clearing and healing work on yourself
- Tibetan singing bowls or other forms of sound healing
- crystal healing, crystal grids, healing crystal jewelry

Lady Roxanna: Is this Mine?

One of the easiest ways to keep your energy clear, especially if you're an empath, is to ask, "Is this energy mine?" If the answer is "no," then release the energy and shake it off. Wiggle your hands and feet and do a little dance if you need to. My personal favorite method is a salt bath. You can use Epsom salts or pink salt, just not table salt. Salt is amazingly cleansing! After I cleaned everyone in the French Quarter (remember all the sneezing?), I took a pink salt bath every day for a week to clear my field. Try to soak for a full twenty minutes and set the intention to release all negative energy as you let it flow down the drain.

Terry: We Are One

I like to **ground** by envisioning myself as one with the Universe, like an infinite spider web where everything is connected. My feet are planted firmly on the ground as I imagine Universal Energy flowing through me in a figure eight, similar to the way blood circulates throughout the body. This clears all the crap energy out and brings in new healthy, vibrant energy. Clearing is vital every time you feel less than optimum. It is even more critical in taxing situations such as: before, during, and after being in a crowd of people; doing a personal reading for someone; and before and after bed. It is easy to absorb other people's energy, so it only makes sense to clear it, right? Kinda like when someone coughs or sneezes near you. You don't want their cooties on you, so you step away or clean up as soon as you can.

I also use a clear-as-I-go method I call **Take 5.** Start by noticing heaviness or denseness in your energy throughout the day. As you notice it, simply acknowledge its presence. You can then remove it by seeing in your mind's eye, then imagining it being cleared, uncreated, eradicated and deleted from your space, place, and existence. This is a fast process which can be completed within the time it takes to deeply inhale and exhale. As you inhale, you are envisioning all the clean healthy energy entering your being, and as you exhale you are imagining all the dense energy being pushed out by the good energy you just inhaled.

#LightworkerProblems

As a Lightworker, you may experience things that ordinary people don't feel or notice. For example:

- Unusual sensitivity to light, noise, smells, etc.
- Aversion to crowds
- Extreme aversion to negative individuals or toxic people
- Headaches and lightheadedness for no apparent reason (HINT: drink more water and ground your energy)
- Getting intuitive "downloads" out of the blue that may or may not make sense to you
- Receiving intuitive guidance that isn't optimal to share. This can leave you thinking, "Okay, so what the heck am I supposed to do with this info?"
- Feeling funky vibes in a space and needing to get out of that space ASAP
- Nausea that resolves as soon as you get away from a certain space or person
- Accidentally knowing things that are supposed to be surprises and secrets
- Getting chills indoors in the summer
- Blowing out light bulbs simply by flipping the switch
- Difficulty sleeping in hotels or away from home

Terry: Trouble with Electricity

My energetic make up responds to anything around me that requires electrical energy to function (watches, cell phones, laptops, lights, etc.). Holding my cell phone in my hand causes it to constantly shut off, freeze up, stall, and just plain wack out. This is pretty dang frustrating when I'm trying to make a call or actually use my phone to do anything productive! I got so angry, sick, and tired of the episodes, I would want to throw it against a wall. My husband thinks this is hilarious and says, "Give it to me." Sure enough, as soon as he has the phone in his hand, it stops its shenanigans. Then he laughs and says, "See, there's nothing wrong with it, it's just you." While I was setting up my website with the webmaster over the phone, I had to have my husband sit next to me the whole time because that guy's server kept crashing and the phone kept cutting off. Power can be a real pain in the ass sometimes!

Amy: Bye-Bye, Surprise Parties

*As an intuitive, you can pretty much say goodbye to surprise parties and surprise gifts. I mean, they still happen, but the surprise element will be wasted on you. My family and friends have tried to surprise me with birthday parties, baby showers, etc., but I always knew it was happening. It's particularly frustrating for my husband, because he says I take all the fun out of gifting! But I'm not **trying** to know these things, the information just comes through, and so I know them.*

Lady Roxanna: Energetic Hitchhikers

*In 2011, my family went to Boston for a wonderful vacation where we went whale watching, walked the Freedom Trail (including graveyards), and visited the historic surgical suite at Massachusetts General Hospital, where the first anesthesia was given. Before we left home, I set the intention for us to have a wonderful time, only meet friendly helpful people, and to return home safely. I never once thought about setting up **protection** during this trip. Upon returning home, we began to snipe at each other. I thought, "What the hell? We had a great trip!" While talking to another healer, he said, "That's not you talking. You brought a ghost home with you." So the other healer and I sent the ghost on his way to the Light. I smudged the house by burning sage and clearing out any remnants of the negativity, and everything went back to normal.*

You can study these things as much as you want, but sometimes on-the-job training is the only way to learn. Our next vacation *the following year was to San Francisco, and I was determined **not** to repeat our previous experience. Before we left for the tour of Alcatraz island, I spent thirty minutes setting up protection for us. I set an intention, asked my angels and guides to watch over us, placed us in a bubble of protection, etc. I may have gone a little overboard but because of where we were going, I wasn't taking any chances.*

We had a lovely day at Alcatraz except my husband got pooped on by a seagull. He was not happy, but someone nearby said it's supposed to be good luck. After the tour we returned to the mainland to enjoy dinner at a popular local restaurant. We didn't have a reservation, and they wouldn't let us sit at the bar because we had our son with us, so they seated us at a counter area where you could watch the cooks preparing the food. We struck up a conversation with the woman next to us, and she asked what else we wanted to do while we were there. My husband said he wanted to go to the Winchester House, and she replied, "I can help you with that." She was a board member for the Winchester House and we scored free tickets plus a gift card for the gift shop! This convinced my husband the seagull really was good luck and the protection certainly didn't hurt. We had a wonderful trip and returned home ghost-free.

Clearing Your Own Resistance

Would it surprise you to know that resistance had to be cleared before we could begin work on this very book? Imagine how many books are never written or published due to resistance. There's an interesting story associated with how this book finally came about, which you can find at the end of this book. Amy and Terry had a bit of resistance to getting this project rolling, and once they began to invite others to collaborate, that's when massive resistance kicked in. Collaborations of any kind bring their own share of challenges and intricacies, and this book was no different. Once the writing team was set, it took months to coax out the first bits of actual writing. Then, about halfway through the process, it became evident that the launch date needed to be moved up, which condensed the entire process and added even more pressure.

From a Lightworker perspective, it can be frustrating when the Divine places demands on us without explanation. We may feel pressured and stressed out as we push harder to meet deadlines set by our often invisible guides. It is often only after the fact, in hindsight, that we become aware of the reasons behind our promptings. In the moment, the only message we receive may simply be, "Do this now." As we've mentioned in previous chapters, this is where we must learn to rely on our guides and to trust the process. The more we understand that our spiritual team has got our backs, the less frustrating the whole process becomes.

But what happens when the intuitive guidance you receive feels like too big of an ask? This is when trust in our guides may feel tested. Practicing regular self-care helps ease those bumps in the road, as does working with another healer, coach, or Lightworker.

Jen: Meditation Keeps Me Steady

Meditation is the most helpful way I continue to move forward as a Lightworker and as a person. As I become more still within myself, it becomes easier for me to show up for the client and remain neutral to whatever information comes through. I recently had a session with a client who is in her thirties and quite ill. During this session, I received information that told me the client would likely only live another three years. I felt the gravity of the information in my body and kept the channel open for more details to come through. I was guided to focus on joy with her, and help her create meaningful, joyful experiences.

My meditation practice helps me to be able to stay centered and not get thrown off by difficult information that surfaces. I am able to stay focused and keep going, without getting caught up in my own emotional reactions to the message. This way, I am able to help my client process information and formulate an action plan. A daily practice of twenty minutes of meditation per day makes a huge difference in my ability to remain stable, so I can witness what is arising and stay in my center.

I also use three essential oils help me to remain positive and solution-oriented during my grief recovery: frankincense, melissa, and copaiba. I take these oils every day and before client sessions to help me get into the zone and stay clear.

Once you become a Lightworker and develop mastery within your skillset, you'll no longer need coaches or healers, right? Not exactly. Just as many therapists and counselors have their own counselor, many Lightworkers find it helpful to have their own coach and/or healer as well. Even once you've become quite skilled at your craft, you may encounter certain situations that feel unknown to you. Likewise, you may find you could use some extra guidance to clear a particularly challenging block or navigate a big life experience. As you grow and expand, you will likely seek out more advanced healers and coaches for guidance.

Jen: Angels Lifted My Load

When I first started working with clients, it was difficult for me not to take on too much of their energy, troubles, and ghosts. With some of my early clients, I would feel tired for two or three days after the session. When I cleared ghosts for clients, they would sometimes come home with me. I began working with a coach who specialized in working with Angels, and she taught me how to open and close a session energetically. The process was simple: I would light a candle, invite in my guides, energetically open the session, invite in the client and their guides, and then we would begin the session. Once the meeting was concluded and the client left, I would thank the guides, ask them to go, blow out the candle, and end the session. I also dry brushed my body to recharge and to more clearly separate my energy system from the energy system of the client. Keeping my workspace free of energetic disturbances and having clear boundaries around the start and end times of sessions was a huge leap forward in my ability to see multiple clients a day. Now I can see many clients each day and come away feeling energized instead of drained.

Benefits of Working with Other Lightworkers

There are many benefits to continuing to work with other healers and Lightworkers. For example:

- Another healer has a more objective perspective on your life and your issues, and therefore, can often heal you more rapidly than you can heal yourself.
- Other healers often have different skillsets than you, providing you with a wider variety of tools for your healing.
- It expands your network of support.
- It reminds you that you are not alone.
- This person can likely receive information for you in a more objective manner than you can for yourself.
- It feels good to know someone else is taking care of you.
- It gives you a break from always being the healer.
- It gives you a new perspective on healing, as you can now see things from the perspective of the receiving end of Lightworking.
- It creates a synergy, unblocks creativity, and gives you new ideas and insights.
- It is a form of self-care and self-love.
- It is sometimes easier to trust information you receive

from another healer than it is to trust information you receive for your own self.

- It is easier to receive difficult news from someone else, as you may be resistant to hearing it directly from your own intuition.
- As a client, you can appreciate the value of a good healer, which in turn makes it easier for you to invite others to pay you for your healing work.
- You may be able to barter services; to give and receive. This can really strengthen a bond and create a lovely new friendship.
- Because sometimes ordering in just feels better and easier than cooking.

Lady Roxanna: Don't Be Afraid to Ask

It's always good to have a healer for yourself to help you with your own stuff. As much as we all like to think, "I can do this all by myself," that's just not true. An unbiased opinion can be as good as gold in helping you heal your own stuff, and I'm telling you this from personal experience. I don't like to ask for help, but sometimes it is necessary and a blessing. Don't be afraid to ask.

Jen: I Have a Team

Right now, I have a handful of practitioners that I can call upon to have a session on an as-needed basis: five life coaches, an intuitive, a yogi, a chiropractor and a Reiki master. I have also been working with a very intuitive grief counselor for 18 months now, which has been incredibly grounding for me. Group workshops and retreats help me to uplevel quickly by gaining new insights and knowledge, and receiving validation from the experiences of others. I have often experienced quantum leaps forward during group work.

Retreats and Workshops

Retreats and workshops are an extraordinary way to expand your own channel while connecting with other Lightworkers. The diversity of group work combines with a short, intense timeframe to build fast bonds and create rapid transformation.

Amy: To the Moon

If working one-on-one with a Lightworker is like learning to fly, then going on a well-crafted retreat is like skyrocketing to the moon. It continues to amaze me how much we're able to clear in such a short period of time, and the transformation is often visible. We really should take before and after photos for each retreat because you can literally see the years and the stress come off of a person's appearance with the work that we do.

Lady Roxanna: Battleground Energy

Retreats are my favorite way to connect with other spiritual people and go to places my soul is calling for me to visit. In 2015, I went on a retreat to Glastonbury, England, and climbed to the top of the TOR tower to connect with Archangel Michael. I stood on the ley lines there, went to the Chalice Well, toured the Goddess Temple, and visited every other high energy spot in town. It was a fabulous experience and I grew tremendously as a person and as a Lightworker.

When the retreat was over, I met up with my best friend Sarah and we went on to Scotland together, which was absolutely amazing! The connection I felt to the land and the people was extraordinary, like coming home to a place I'd never been. We took a private tour of Culloden Battlefield, where the energy was beyond intense. I could feel the energy from the ground and, depending on where we were standing, we could feel the subtle nuances between the different energies. Some were easier to take than others. My connection to this place was certain, and seeing the family names on the marker rocks was profound for me.

In the next chapter, we'll continue to dive deeper into your next steps as a Lightworker. But first, why not take a few minutes to complete your Food for Thought questions?

Chapter 7 Food for Thought

1. Review the list of ways to keep your energy clean on page 100 and highlight the examples that interest you. Choose one you've never heard of and take some time to research how to use it. Implement this new tool and see whether it resonates with you.

2. Can you recall a time when you were having a great day and feeling good and then suddenly you felt sick or your mood shifted? Did you notice, or did someone else notice? How did it make you feel? What did you do about it? Knowing what you've learned so far about Lightworkers and subtle energies, can you look back and identify whether or not the experience of that shift belonged to you?

3. Are you open to working with other healers? Explore the reasons why or why not.

Chapter 8:

Honing Your Craft

Wait, didn't we already talk about this? We've explored how to advance along the learning curve, why it's helpful to work with other coaches and healers, why the learning journey never ends, and the benefits of retreats and connections with other Lightworkers. Do we really need another chapter on this?

Oh Sweet One, the fun has only just begun! Such is the journey of a Lightworker. Remember how we said we never truly "arrive"? If getting to the core of an issue is like peeling off layers of an onion, then living into Lightworking is like making baklava. You just keep adding layer after layer of buttery, flaky phyllo dough until it's time to bake it and eat it. Okay, so the food analogies aren't always precise, since it sounds like we're saying eating means dying, but you get the idea, right? Growing and developing yourself as a Lightworker on this planet is a multi-layered process. Your next step is to take the modalities you've started exploring and working with, and develop these skills into mastery.

The Road to Mastery

Malcolm Gladwell claims it takes approximately 10,000 hours of focused practice in order to become masterful at anything. That's right, according to information in his 2008 book, *Outliers,* you could become a master chef right now. All you have to do is train, focus, and cook full time for the next five years. NOTE: microwaving three meals a day doesn't count.

Once you become proficient at something, the next logical step is mastery. Not everyone wants to achieve mastery, of course. You may already know how to cook at a level that is satisfactory to you. How many of the contestants from *Worst Cooks in America* do you think go on to become professional chefs? We're guessing very few, if any. Sometimes being proficient is sufficient.

Yet, when it comes to Lightworking, we haven't seen this to be the case. Many of the Lightworkers we know and love seem to have insatiable appetites for improving their abilities and expanding their skillsets. Perhaps it is our inherent desire to serve all of humankind; or possibly it's our desire to achieve enlightenment; or maybe it just feels good to get better and better.

Whatever the reason, we Lightworkers tend to be a "dive deep" kind of bunch. If your discovery phase in Chapter 3 was about going wide and exploring as many aspects of Lightworking that interested you, then the focus in this step is about going deep into just one or two specific methods and modalities, becoming as good as you possibly can at these. This increases your effectiveness as a Lightworker, builds your confidence, and positions you as an expert.

Amy: Get Clear. Get Results.

As a master intuitive healer, I help people to get clear. We start by gaining clarity, as in being "clear" about where they are, where they want to be, and what's in their way. Then we clear or remove their blocks, doubts, fears, and limitations so that their path is free from obstruction and they can move forward swiftly and powerfully. When I first started out, I wanted to do it all, to be everything for everyone. "Just bring me wherever you're blocked and we'll heal it," I thought. I learned the hard way that this isn't how life is meant to work, and neither is Lightworking.

*Once I narrowed my focus to "getting clear," I attracted more clients with greater ease, and my specific purpose and area of expertise became crystal clear. Isn't that funny? I myself had to first get clear about clarity, before I could help people to get clear. My guides are not without a sense of humor! As of today, I've published ten books and my writing has appeared in countless other books, periodicals, and online sources. Once I knew **how** I could help people, the books started writing themselves and the pace quickened.*

Working with a Mentor

Where can you go to hone your craft? Seek out the very best teachers and healers and work with them as closely as you can. We're inviting you to branch out now, well beyond books and blogs. Find leaders and healers you resonate with, and figure out how you can get into their presence to learn as much as you can from them. Now is the time to find your mentor! Read the author bios at the end of this book and reach out to those you feel you connect with.

The healers, guides, and Lightworkers you admire now won't be around forever, at least not physically. We recently lost

Louise Hay, founder of Hay House Publishing and author of many books including *You Can Heal Your Life*. Louise Hay was a pioneer in the world of self-healing and understanding the underlying metaphysical reasons for physical ailments. She is gone from our world now, and while she has touched many lives and left behind an amazing legacy, we no longer have the opportunity to be in her physical presence, to listen to her speak as part of a live audience, or to learn directly from her intuitive wisdom.

What's more, some of the Lightworkers you love today will continue to amass their following, which means they'll soon be less affordable and less accessible for one-on-one mentoring. If you feel moved to work with someone directly, go with that; don't hesitate. Attend their workshops and retreats; sign up for their one-on-one coaching and mentoring and healing work; and find out how you can connect with them personally. Make a list of your questions and anything you need clarified. Expect that you can and will get those answers and clarifications. Be bold and be daring. Commit to your craft and believe in yourself. Yes, it's an investment. Yes, it may seem expensive. But it is the smartest, most efficient way for you to get better at the modalities you've chosen (or that have chosen you).

Terry: Today, We're Like Family

My drive for learning is insatiable. As long as I learn at least one new thing a day, I am ecstatic. I am always reading, writing, taking classes, courses, training, and anything else I can do to have more, be more, and do more. After educating myself for so many years, I knew I was ready for a mentor, and that's when I encountered the Spiritual Ass Kicker, Amy Scott Grant. Working one-on-one with Amy gave me the confidence and knowledge I needed to start my businesses. Today, we are more than successful entrepreneurs together—Amy and I have become like family.

Pushing Your Edges

As you shift from proficiency to mastery, your confidence will finally begin to soar. With practice and continued growth, you'll be able to remain calmer and more connected during sessions, and your trust level with your inner guidance will increase exponentially.

And yet…

A funny thing happens as your confidence grows as a Lightworker. New experiences and unexpected life twists start pushing your edges, stretching you to your very limits. Many Lightworkers have felt like they've reached their breaking point at some point in their journey.

Terry: My One-Sided Yelling Match with God

For years, I felt my energy was pushed past my limit to the point where it felt like it was affecting my heartbeat. It started out small, like riding a roller coaster, but then it progressed to bouts of feeling anxious. Then it felt like my heart was going to jump out of my chest while taking my breath away. Some days it would go on all day and other days there would be a break for a few or more days. There was no method to the madness, no discernable pattern or relief. This racing energy got so bad, it started to affect equipment I worked with at the hospital. This went on for many years, and I was angry that my annual physical never uncovered any heart problems or any sign of what was going on. Finally, I got so mad that I started yelling at God while in my car. I screamed at Him: "This is B.S.! How can anyone conduct their lives like this?!" and on and on. Shortly after this one-sided yelling match, I discovered that all I had to do was ask for a break and it would be granted. Well, duh. After another one-side yelling match with God at a later date, I screamed at him to "fix this or else." A few months later, all the symptoms disappeared in a wink. The moral of the story is to ask for something when it bothers you or when you feel you are unable to handle it. You know, maybe before it gets to the point where you want to scream.

Amy: Psychic Attack

After I had been a healer for several months, something went wrong. I suddenly found myself feeling angry and irritated all the time, for no reason whatsoever. Remember how Harry felt when Voldemort had started to invade his mind and the occlumency lessons from Snape just weren't working? Yeah, it was just like that.

*When my pendulum started giving me wonky answers, I didn't know what to do so I called up a Lightworker friend who told me I had a negative entity attached to my energy field. WTF?! I thought. No one told me **that** was a possibility. I didn't sign any waiver, and I wasn't aware of the risks and potential dangers associated with this Lightworking stuff. The first Lightworker couldn't make the entity go away, which left me feeling frustrated, hopeless, and abandoned.*

A couple of days later, while soaking in a hot bath, I found myself darkly wondering what would happen if my hair dryer fell into the tub while it was still plugged in. I noticed this thought and immediately got out of the bath for self-preservation. Holy crap, I thought. This thing is trying to snuff me out! I called a different Lightworker friend who came to my rescue. He cleared the entity from my field, removed all the entities and negative energy from my house, and set up a coning of protection around my home and property.

Years later, while reading about psychic attack, I understood that's what had happened to me. It was a horrible experience I wouldn't wish on my worst enemy, but I'm grateful I can recognize it in a heartbeat now.

What About Protection?

There are many ways to keep yourself safe while performing energy work. For starters, *do not* watch the 1999 Kevin Bacon supernatural horror flick, *Stir of Echoes*. Instead, you may wish to try any of these methods:

- envision yourself in a column of Divine white light from the Universe to the core of the earth
- set and hold the intention that only Divine energy is allowed into your space/session
- invite in your guardian angels and the angels of the person you're working on (if applicable)
- ask Archangel Michael to place his golden dome of protection over you as you begin a session
- surround yourself in a bubble of Divine white healing light and energy
- ground yourself and your physical space before doing energy work
- a more advanced method is to dial up the light within you and radiate your field outward

Some Lightworkers promote the use of protective grids and energetic structures, but in our experience, these are short-lived and ineffective against the big guns. Additionally, adding layers of protection around your energetic field can have the unwanted side effect of barriers to intimacy, feeling walled off from others, and weight gain. Besides which, there are certain inevitable life experiences against which protective energy is ineffective.

Jen: Mom, I'm Here

Losing my son Oliver to cancer shook my confidence as a Lightworker. I had worried about him getting cancer since he was two years old. I did everything I knew to do: I shopped at

Whole Foods, eliminated toxic cleaners, lived away from high tension power lines, fretted about indoor air quality, bought organic cotton sheets, and made sure our furniture finishes were arsenic free. We ate clean and took high quality supplements. I worked as hard as I possibly could to prevent him from getting cancer. And when he did, I worked as hard as I could to explore every possible solution on the planet for terminal cancer.

I felt certain that being an intuitive and trusting in hosts of Archangels and angels would save my son. When it did not— when he died—I was utterly disillusioned. I felt that the past 13 years of my life had been a complete waste of time and a delusion. I became more invested in three-dimensional reality and pulled back from intuition. Which probably would have worked, except that my son now exists in the fifth dimension.

About eight months after losing him, I went to see a gifted intuitive who channels loved ones for people. I was hoping, begging for Oliver to come through. It was the first time since he died that I had opened up and asked the angels for help. I felt a warm tingling glow around me, and the whole vibration of my body shifted. A few seconds later I heard Oliver's voice whisper, "Mom, mom, mom, I'm here." Almost instantly, the intuitive noticed him and gave me a beautiful message from him. At that moment, I realized how much I had missed being in the flow of energy and being carried by the Divine. That was the beginning of my path to forgiveness, love, transcendence, and grace.

This is why we encourage you to build your support network to include fellow coaches, healers, intuitives, and energy workers. Self-care is vital as well, because the more you take care of your own wellness and emotional well-being, the better equipped you are to handle each new and challenging curveball life throws your way. As you heal and recover, the experience and growth you've endured further deepens your abilities as a Lightworker.

Jen: Strength and Steadiness

Returning to work as a yoga teacher, healer, life coach, artist, and essential oils team leader after losing my son to cancer has been a powerful and humbling experience. People share huge problems with me within the first five minutes of a session, and they drop right into trusting me with the heaviness of their challenges. I'm not sure I had the strength and steadiness to help people with sobering and painful truths until now.

Apply What You Learn

One caveat here is to ensure you don't get stuck in perpetual learning mode, as this can cause you to remain inside your comfort zone, gathering information but not stepping out into the world to share it and do your good work. Some Lightworkers find themselves in a cycle of feeling as though they need to "learn more" before they can truly step into the role of healer or coach or guide. At some point, it's best to decide to leave the safety nest of perpetual student and apply what you learn in real life. After all, the world is waiting for your gifts.

Lady Roxanna: Psychic Soup

I am a student of life, and have been that way all my life. My father used to tease me by saying I was going to be a professional student, which meant I was not ever going to go to work. He lovingly afforded me that luxury. I hold two college degrees plus many certifications and modalities that I work with and use with my clients. I am a "seeker of truth" as evidenced by my astrological chart and my Human Design chart. I seek not only for my own knowledge but to share with the world. I am sharing some of my experiences with you now, so that you can be prepared and have some idea of what to expect. Be aware it is changing and speeding up all the time, so you can expect to learn faster and adapt more quickly.

As you learn, you will take bits and pieces of things and create your own "psychic soup." Use the things that work for you and leave the rest behind, and whatever you become good at will soon become your strengths. Someone very wise recently told me it was selfish to hoard all this knowledge I have attained, and it is time to share it with the world. May we all use it to be a beacon of light in this world.

Chapter 8 Food for Thought

1. What will it take for you to transition from proficiency to mastery? Do you have any fears or concerns about this? Are you willing to progress in spite of these?

2. What (if any) blocks or resistance do you notice around working closely with a Lightworker as a mentor?

3. Write down at least one or two Lightworking modalities that seem natural or easy for you. Consider these to be the ones you hone and master first.

Chapter 9:

Fear of Exposure

If you woke up one day, realized you were a Lightworker, and immediately emailed all your family and friends, then good for you! That definitely puts you in the minority among Lightworkers. For most of us, it's been an "aw, crap" kind of experience, followed by, "Oh no! What is so-and-so going to think?"

Fear of exposure is something most of us have experienced as Lightworkers, and even as you read this, you might still find yourself unwilling to come out of the spiritual closet just yet. Please know that wherever you are now is fine. Remember, this book is here to provide you with your next steps as you emerge as a Lightworker. There's no set timetable for this process, it's really just up to you.

Lady Roxanna: Practice Brings Ease

I had fears about going public, especially before doing that first reading. I was so worried I wouldn't get anything. Truly, this has never happened to me, but that doesn't mean the fear goes away! I always start with a prayer asking for the highest and best to come through, and it has never let me down. I have had people tell me I give amazing readings when I just trust what comes through and share that with the client. The more you practice, the easier it becomes, and gaining confidence in your abilities makes it easier still.

Reasons for Fear of Exposure

We hold onto this fear of exposure for many reasons, some of which may surprise you. See if any of the following resonate. Or better yet—use your pendulum or Truth Testing to check and see which of the following applies to you:

- You had a past life as a Lightworker (witch, shaman, witch doctor, intuitive, psychic, astrologer, etc.) that didn't end well. Perhaps you were hung, burned at the stake, outcast, etc.
- You worry your religious family and close friends will not accept you.
- Your religious upbringing makes you want to keep it quiet.
- You hold "fraud energy" in your field, likely from a past life as a snake oil salesman, or a similar experience.
- In a past life, you had great abilities and corresponding power that you abused or misused, and people got hurt.
- Someone died because of your gifts in a past life.
- You shared your private gifts and abilities with someone, who then betrayed or "outed" you, which could have occurred in this lifetime or in a past life.
- You gave someone an intuitive message but then things went terribly wrong.
- You were hurt/abandoned/betrayed for sharing your gifts in a past life.

Amy: No One Is Gunning for Me

I can't tell you how many times I've cleared the same flavor of fear of exposure for different clients. It played out like this: they had special gifts in a past life, which they kept private. One day they take a risk to help someone in need, which turns out to be the very person who betrays them. As a result, they get caught and die. Like all our favorite Hollywood films, it's the same basic story, over and over. No wonder we're afraid to open up shop and call ourselves healers! The history and prior consequences still haunt us from the shadows. Once we finally get these cleared and resolved, we are able to fully step into our gifts with fear or trepidation. I can literally remember the liberation I felt the day I finally realized, "Wow! No one is gunning for me! I'm free!"

Most Lightworkers have had to clear and release a certain amount of blocks, fears, and past life hurts before we could "go public" with our gifts. This stage can cause anxiety and tension, and it's best to work with a gifted healer who can help you to clear and resolve this super old stuff, so you can be free to move forward and share your work with the world.

Jen: Approval Matters Less

Needing my parents to be proud of me and approve of what I was doing was a huge challenge for me initially. I still don't talk much with my parents about my work. They no longer hassle me to baptize my children or have any hopes that I will come back to the church. We don't talk about religion or spiritual beliefs when we see each other. In my heart I know that God, the Divine, Infinite Wisdom, whatever name we give it, wants us all to feel unconditionally loved, happy, and free. I also know that I am open to choose whatever pathway brings me closest to God. As I've grown in my work and stand in it more powerfully, I know that I've been able to help a lot of people, so it matters less who approves of my work and who doesn't. I know that I am serving people in my unique way, and that is enough for me.

It's true that not all of us are here to earn our living as a paid Lightworker. But holding onto fears of exposure are detrimental to all Lightworkers (as well as to those we are here to serve), not just to those who decide to make it their profession. Fear keeps us stuck and hidden, which serves no one. We are here to share, not to hide. Our Lightworker's Guide private community is a great place to start:

TheLightworkersGuide.com

Terry: We've Come a Long Way, Baby

We have come a long way since the dark ages when it comes to expressing ourselves as an Intuitive, Psychic, Tarot Reader, Witch, Astrologer, or whatever label you prefer. People are no longer hanged for having special intuitive healing gifts. In fact, more and more Lightworkers are now being paid handsomely for their gifts and abilities. Look at Sylvia Brown, Edgar Cayce, Uri Gellar, and John Edwards, for example.

However, many Lightworkers remain afraid of putting themselves out there, worried about what other people think. Even still, there are earning opportunities as a telephone reader or in an obscure local metaphysical shop. Others like myself "clear the fear" of exposure so we can get out there and help others just like you to do the same. It is for this reason this very book came to be! You may choose to be that Lightworker who stays hidden, and that is fine as long as you know that anything is possible once you clear the fear.

Sometimes the very worst experiences in life can yield exquisite gifts and abilities for us. As we are able to work through our own pain and loss, we ultimately grow and expand, which allows us to serve others in an even greater capacity. It makes us even more impactful as Lightworkers.

Jen: My Best Remedy

I know a lot of moms who have lost children through the years who still struggle to find meaning in their lives. Being able to talk to my son on the other side has accelerated my healing process. On many days, I now feel happy to wake up and be alive. I feel interested in and excited about the day. The intuitive process has been incredibly helpful in my healing journey with Oliver. Connecting with him intuitively is one of the greatest remedies, the greatest tools that I have for soothing any fear or resistance that arises when I think about stepping into my work at a greater scale.

Lady Roxanna: Out of the Shadows

I have known for a long time that I am a healer and I am here to do this work, but fear kept me in the shadows. I honestly don't know the number of times I have been persecuted in past lives for being a healer, witch, or wise woman. No wonder so many healers have throat issues! We are afraid to speak our truth because we have suffered and been killed so many times in the past, just for being our authentic selves.

I have done lots of personal work around this issue to clear these blocks for myself so that I can come forward and step into my power. Remember, you always have a choice. You can choose to say no or ignore your gift, but it won't go away; it always comes back. I can no longer ignore mine, because everything I have been asking for is starting to happen. Of course, that doesn't mean I don't still have fears. I do, but I started with baby steps and it's growing from there. My name is Lady Roxanna and I know I am a healer.

Choosing when to step forward and bring your gifts to the world is a very personal decision indeed. For many of us, this occurs when the cost of staying hidden in the shadows becomes greater than the cost of stepping out into the light. However, it will be important to resolve any fears of exposure before continuing on to your next step: going public.

Chapter 9 Food for Thought

1. Remember the list of fears at the beginning of this chapter? Refer to that list as you write here all the fears you feel. You may also wish to add more. Next, evaluate each fear one at a time and see if you can determine the origin.

2. For each of the fears you wrote in your answer above, ask yourself: is this a legitimate concern, or can I simply choose to let this go? Let go of all the ones you can, and for the rest, make the commitment now to clear those remaining fears.

3. Do you believe you can make a good living doing what you love and what you're good at? If you answered no, clear those limiting beliefs. If you answered yes, consider this: do you want to? What other beliefs might you have to give up or let go of in order to earn a comfortable living (or better) as a Lightworker?

Chapter 10:

Going Public

Believe it or not, some Lightworkers—many in fact, never go public with their gifts. Amy knows a physician who does Reiki on all of his patients via their charts, before they even walk into his office. She once asked him if he planned to open a Reiki practice once he retired from medicine. His reply was short and clear: "Nope." There are many reasons why a Lightworker might choose to keep their gifts private, and they're not all fear-based. Consider these, for a start:

- don't want the publicity
- don't like the spotlight or being the center of attention
- prefer to work behind the scenes in a support role
- don't like money
- don't feel they should be paid for their work
- don't need or want money
- afraid of success
- afraid of failure

- prefer to serve in other ways
- prefer to be a "secret weapon" of love and light
- don't have any support from their family or friends
- don't realize that a healing business is an option
- don't believe people would pay for their gifts
- prefer to use their gifts as a way to give back
- don't want to give up their day job
- still have blocks around coming out of the spiritual closet
- have other reasons for staying in their current career
- prefer to view Lightworking as a hobby
- don't believe they're good enough
- don't think they've learned enough yet or had enough practice
- tried to go public but didn't like it or it didn't work
- it's not their calling to take their gifts public

Once you decide to go public, that may or may not mean you're launching yourself as a Lightworking entrepreneur. For you, "going public" may simply mean you're not afraid to tell people what you can do. For many Lightworkers, it takes some time and careful thought to figure out what to call themselves, and how to explain exactly what they do. The Food for Thought questions at the end of this chapter will help you begin to clarify your explanation for your gifts. In the meantime, ponder this:

How do you see yourself helping people as a Lightworker?

How do you receive information? Do you see it, hear it, know it, feel it, or do you use tools like cards or crystals to discover and receive?

Do you see yourself as a healer? Have you helped someone heal physically, emotionally, mentally, or spiritually through your Lightworker abilities?

Jen: Reinvention

It's an interesting challenge to come up with a name for what we do, and I'm in the process of it myself. Every client session I've had since returning to work after losing my son to cancer feels ten or twenty times more powerful than the sessions I used to have, whether it's Reiki, Rising Star, or playing my gong for sound healing. I am awestruck by the clarity of the information I now receive, so any marketing or self-definition I had before doesn't quite cover what I'm doing now. I'm in a complete space of reinvention.

Many of us have found it helpful to choose a name or a title as a way to clarify what we do, and to create a conversation opener. When someone asks you, "So, what do you do?" it's important to have a clear and concise answer, like an "elevator speech." Practice yours to ensure it sounds and feels entirely comfortable to you. That way, whenever someone asks you, it can flow off your tongue freely, easily, and understandably. You may even want to test out a few titles, phrases, or elevator pitches to see which ones feel the best to you in a real conversation.

Some Lightworkers prefer to invent a witty phrase to describe themselves, whereas others simply state their name and what they do. Still others choose a new name, or a variant of their name. For example:

> Sylvia Celeste Browne ~ Author, Psychic, and
>   Spiritual Medium
> Edgar Cayce ~ American mystic
> Uri Geller ~ Illusionist, Magician, and
>   Self-Proclaimed Psychic
> John Edward ~ Psychic Medium
> Lady Roxanna

Amy: Spiritual Ass Kicker

When I started doing healing work, Lightworkers generally weren't funny, and they definitely didn't swear all over the place like I do. I knew I needed a title that would give people a heads up that we were gonna kick ass in a fun and an irreverent way. That's when "Spiritual Ass Kicker" popped in. Over the years, I've considered changing it for various reasons but so far, nothing else resonates as strongly. It's proven to be an all-or-nothing conversation starter. Those who are interested in what I do perk up when I say it and start asking me questions right away…and it halts the energy of those who are not interested (or perhaps even offended), leaving us both free to change topics or move on and engage with someone else. They way I look at, life's too short to stand around talking to someone you simply don't resonate with. I'd rather spend that time getting to know someone interesting and open-minded.

Don't Get Married to a Title

Some Lightworkers seem to remain stuck in this stage, uncertain what to call themselves and therefore unable to move forward. Just as Jen shared how she's reinventing and redefining her work in the wake of losing her son, the same happens to any Lightworker who undergoes a major life transition. Our gifts morph as we shift, which means we may need to eventually change the name for what we do.

Keep this in mind: you're not making a forever commitment with whatever title or name you choose. Sure, whenever you change it you might have to make a couple of edits on your website, but replacement business cards are cheap and besides, you're worth it.

Some Lightworkers avoid titles and labels entirely, but if you're considering becoming a paid Lightworker, it's important to be able to succinctly describe how you can help people.

Otherwise, how can they find you and/or recognize you as the person who can help them?

Once you've figured out what to call yourself and/or what you can do for people, the next step is to put yourself out there. We generally recommend taking small, consistent baby steps to acclimate yourself to this process. If you were just learning to cook, you probably wouldn't start by making Beef Wellington and chocolate soufflé, would you? Nah, you would start by learning to properly cut vegetables and raw ingredients, and then move up to more challenging dishes. You probably wouldn't begin to think of yourself as a cook or a chef until you had achieved a certain level of mastery. But once you can slice and dice with consistency and speed, and you've got a handle on certain cuisines and flavor profiles, how would you respond when someone asks if you can cook? Would you bat your eyes bashfully and mumble, "a little." Or would you smile and say, "Yes, I love to cook. Are you hungry?" Or would your response be somewhere in-between?

Guess what? There's no right answer! Your response depends on your confidence level, your comfort level in talking to new people, and your personality. But know this: no one can eat your food if they don't even know that you can cook. Likewise, no one can benefit from your abilities if you never tell anyone what you can do.

Terry: Out There and Empowered

It took me some time to figure out how to address myself with the gifts I have. I still change it up occasionally, just because I can. Originally, I referred to myself as a New Life Mentor, Healer & Intuitive Lightworker. Currently, I refer to myself as an Intuitive Advisor, Healer, & Whole Being Enhancement Specialist. I put myself out there as soon as my website went live, and I immediately started sharing on social media. Sure, I had some apprehension around it at first, but as soon as I cleared that fear and just did it, I felt empowered and was able to mentor others to do the same.

Putting yourself out there is first and foremost about believing that you are who you say you are, and believing that you can do what you say you can do. This is why we've encouraged you in previous chapters to begin practicing on other people, and then to continue to develop and hone your craft. Working with others allows you to build your confidence and really see what you can do. When another person is blown away by your insights or healing abilities, you can't sit in your room alone and think, "Oh, that didn't happen. I must have imagined it all." You've got a first-hand witness to your gift! The more you practice, the more confident you will become, because the more people you will have helped and after all, isn't helping people the very best part of being a Lightworker?

Terry: Bliss, Baby!

My first official paying client was such a high point. I was on a natural energetic high for what seemed like forever. Talk about BLISS! Prior to that I was always helping people, but never asking for anything in return. My husband would get so irritated that I would give away so much of my time without being compensated for all that time that was taken away from the family. It's so rewarding to be able to do what you love while helping people. Getting paid for it is the icing on the cake.

So, What Do You Do?

Today, there are many ways to begin to put yourself out there. The easiest way is to start answering the "So, what do you do?" question with your new Lightworker answer instead of your usual day job answer. You might also wish to update your social media profiles, or create new accounts specifically for those you can assist with your Lightworking. A slightly bigger step is to print up business cards or mini flyers and check out your local metaphysical shops and yoga studios. Even bigger steps include putting up a website, starting a blog, or launching a YouTube channel. Don't let yourself get overwhelmed by the choices, just start small and build from there. Yes, it takes energy and resources to get going, but you'll be glad you started.

Remember in earlier chapters how we talked at length about building trust with your guides and with your inner knowing? Now we'd like to remind you to rely on your guides for support. Know that you can trust and lean on them whenever you need to. Think of it like this: you've got an entourage at your disposal, and they're just waiting to be asked. Is the Executive Chef the only one in the kitchen? No way! There are line cooks, a pastry chef, a saucier, the sous chef, and more. And they're just making dinner, not changing the world! You have many more resources available at your disposal, so use them. Don't fall into the trap of thinking the world is on your shoulders. Ask your guides for help and watch what happens.

Amy: Well, Looky Here!

I fell ass-backwards into my first paid client. Back in 2005, I knew about the Law of Attraction and little else, but I was ready to put myself out there as a coach, so I set myself up energetically to receive. I allocated time for not-yet-enrolled clients on my calendar, I put the words "new coaching clients" up on my vision board, and I decided to start introducing myself as a coach. A friend soon called us to say he and his girlfriend were on a road trip and had just realized they would be driving right through our town, and were we free to meet up for lunch? We were, and we did. Turns out, the girlfriend and I hit it off like only kindred spirits can, and when they were leaving, she turned to me and said, "Wow. I really enjoyed meeting you. I wish I could just pay you to talk to you." Thankfully, I was able to recognize the fulfillment of my wish, so without appearing too flustered I said, "Well, as a matter of fact, I'm a spiritual *coach and I'd love to work with you." I could hardly believe the words myself as I heard them coming out of my mouth. She wrote me a check on the spot and I was officially a paid coach. It's amazing to me what happens once we declare ourselves to **be** something. It's at if the Universe is just waiting for us to be clear and bold and specific, so that it can serve up our every wish.*

Our time together in this book is nearly complete, and you now have all the tools you need to move forward and grow into your role as a Lightworker. Even if today is not the day that you're stepping out into the world, the day is coming. Know that when it does, you will be ready, and you will shine radiantly. Your guides, your invisible entourage, and we four authors will be here, cheering you onward and upward and beaming with delight at the positive difference you make in our world.

Lady Roxanna: Let's Connect

I have studied many different modalities and I use what feels appropriate for each client. Now it is time for me to share it with the world. It is still a work in progress, and I'm learning all the time—working on a website, writing this book, and planning all my future goals. The most important thing is for me to do this work and make myself happy. I am here to give, love, and serve, and my intention is to do just that while I travel the world, helping others and myself. I look forward to meeting some of you on one of my future retreats, or at a live event.

Chapter 10 Food for Thought

1. What are your specific gifts so far as a Lightworker? How do you feel these can best serve people? Who would you most love to help with your abilities?

2. If you had only 7 words to explain what you can do as a Lightworker, what would you say? How does it feel to say that out loud?

3. What are you most concerned would happen if you told someone what you do as a Lightworker? In other words, what is the worst-case scenario? How likely is that to happen? Are you willing to move forward in spite of this small risk?

Chapter 11:

When Relationships Shift

An interesting phenomenon occurs when we step into our roles as Lightworkers and our energy begins to shift. We soon notice that our relationships also shift, and not always in the direction we'd prefer. Friends can suddenly act strangely toward us, demonstrating resentment and frustration, and conflict can crop up in our closest relationships. Amy refers to this as the "relationship gap."

Amy: The Relationship Gap

Ah, the dreaded "relationship gap." This is what occurs when one person in a relationship shifts or grows but the other person doesn't. Now a gap has formed between these two people, and relationship gaps are uncomfortable—especially when living inside the same home. In order to sustain the relationship, the gap must be closed or at least narrowed to a tolerable amount. Either one person steps up and grows, or the other person slides back and reverts. Sure, from the outside it's easy to say what "should" happen, but it's an entirely different animal when you're one of the parties inside the relationship.

With Lightworkers, our growth can be rapid and exponential and if we're not careful, we can leave our partners (and some close friends) behind in the dust. It takes patience and compassion to encourage our loved ones to grow with us. They may not understand or share our calling as Lightworkers, but in order to remain in the relationship they must grow to meet us. Believe me, you don't want to backslide. Nobody wants to be the person who realizes she has unlimited potential, and then one day decides nope, I'm really okay working at a job I hate for too little pay and pretending life is just hard. Here's the rub: if they won't budge, and you won't backslide, then the gap will continue to grow and the relationship will ultimately terminate. Often this is for the best, though that's difficult to appreciate while it's happening.

When relationships get uncomfortable or ultimately end, it can feel like a buzzkill to your Lightworker natural high. Kind of like learning how to prepare an amazing cheesecake for the love of your life only to discover she's just been diagnosed as lactose intolerant. We wonder, "Why can't they just be happy for me?" Because Sweet One, they're not on the same path of love and acceptance as you are. They look at you and think, "What's her/his problem? Why is (s)he so different? All these changes are making me uncomfortable, and I don't like this. Why can't we just go back to the way it was before?"

Jen: I Was Devastated

*I remember living in Virginia while studying to become a yoga teacher. One of my closest friends at the time was a strict Baptist who told me that Jesus did **not** want me to become a yoga teacher. I remember feeling hurt and devastated because she* *was one of my closest friends outside of my yoga community. At that point, I began to realize my work and my unique worldview (which wasn't necessarily aligned with more common worldviews) was likely to create painful experiences for me. It took me a while to get used to the fact that my friendships would shift and change as I kept moving forward.*

Ultimately, letting go of relationships that no longer resonate is what opens the space for new, more aligned relationships to grow and develop. We cannot grow into our new selves and our new truth if we continue to cling to the past and to what no longer serves us. Yes, it is difficult to let go of spouses, partners, friends, and mentors. We have a history together, and there are so many memories and still so much love. But letting go is ultimately part of this circle of life.

Jen: Oliver is Our Common Ground

Knowing that my son Oliver is still in our lives, albeit in a very different way, is immensely important to me. I simply can't be friends with someone who would dismiss the messages I receive from him as coincidences or fiction. That would be too painful for me. People I now choose as close friends have healed from trauma, developed a unique and in-depth spiritual perspective and experience, and are very open to intuitive skills. Our common ground is that we seek to engage in activities that evolve human consciousness.

My parents still have only the vaguest idea of my spiritual beliefs, my work with guides and angels, and my faith in a fifth-dimensional reality. I seldom talk about these topics with my two brothers as well. My sister often tells me how she and her family can sense when my son Oliver is with them whenever they find a shiny penny, or when a half-empty cereal box falls in the pantry. Her daughter has a powerful ability to know when Oliver is nearby. It brings me great comfort to know that my sister's family can sense Oliver with them and know that he is there.

Where can you meet new like-minded people? You can refer back to Chapter 5 where we listed all the places where you can find spiritual folks to practice on. These are the same places that are ideal for meeting new people and growing your Lightworker support network. Yes, even if you live in the middle of nowhere and think you're the only person like you for miles around. For starters, come join our Lightworker's Guide private community:

TheLightworkersGuide.com

Amy: Intention Does It

For a long time, I had only superficial friends nearby. Everyone I worked with and connected with on a deeply spiritual level was miles away, scattered across the country. The upside to this was that any time I wanted to travel, I had friends all over the world to visit and to stay with. But the downside was, I had no spiritual friends near me to take to lunch, or to meet for coffee, or share a walk in the park. One day I realized, oh my God, I'm lonely! I have friends, but none are nearby, and I want people I can hang out with in person and talk about all the crazy things that Lightworkers see and know and do every day. But it feels like everyone in my town is Mormon, so what's a Spiritual Ass Kicker to do? I stopped making excuses and set the intention and all of a sudden spiritual folks were popping up everywhere. They were finding me in the park, in the grocery store, and even at my kids' school. Where had all these people been hiding all this time? They weren't hiding at all of course, but on some level, I suppose I was. Pretty soon, there were too many—more than I could handle, so I turned off the intention and decided to focus on cultivating deeper friendships with some of the local spiritual peeps I'd already met. No matter where you live, you can find your peeps. Just ask your guides for help and expect them to deliver. Even if you're living in the biggest Mormon-town outside of Salt Lake City.

The Company You Keep

You will likely become more selective about the company you keep. It's exhausting to deny our true nature, and to go from small talk conversation to small talk conversation. We Lightworkers crave depth and intimacy. We witness some bizarre shizzle, and it's ever so helpful to be connected with others who understand our unique role, and who've seen some of the same things we've seen.

As you continue to increase your awareness and support your own growth, be mindful in your relationships. Be patient with your non-Lightworker connections, and be patient with yourself. Love and honor yourself, your body, and your work. Listen to those yearnings for rest, rejuvenation, and chocolate. Be good to yourself and lean on your guides. Truth test when you feel confused or uncertain. Speak your truth and be willing to trust.

Lady Roxanna: Energy in the Bank

The most important thing I can share with you is to treat your energy like your bank account. Your energy is a precious resource, so be careful how you spend it. Being on this journey as an energy worker, you will learn to become more selective of the people you call friends, as well as the places you spend your time. Crowds and crowded areas may not be much fun, as you will feel the drain in your energy. I'm not telling you not to do something if you really want to do it; just be prepared that you will probably have to do some energy cleanup afterwards. Like shaking off other people's energy, taking your salt bath, grounding and releasing, or anything else that works for you.

Burning sage or "smudging" is an excellent way to clear your space and clear negative energy from your field. You simply light the sage bundle with a match or lighter and as it begins to smoke, you trace the smoke around your body, not forgetting the bottoms of your feet while holding an intention of energetic cleansing. When you are done, make sure the sage is safely snuffed out, and you can save it for the next time you need it. All of these things are meant to protect your energetic boundaries from other energies. Boundaries are a vital tool in protecting yourself as a Lightworker.

And remember:

It is what it is.

Chapter 11 Food for Thought

1. Which relationships do you have currently that feel supportive and expansive? What thoughts, feelings, and emotions come up for you as you write this?

2. Which relationships feel restrictive or unsupportive to you? Which ones have the biggest "relationship gap"? At this point, do you feel the other person would be willing to grow to meet you, or do you feel the gap is getting wider?

3. How do you think your relationships (both supportive and unsupportive) will impact your experience as a Lightworker? How does your answer make you feel?

Glossary of Terms

NOTE: *This glossary only references terms mentioned inside this book; it is not meant to be a comprehensive glossary for all of Lightworking.*

acupuncture – an alternative healing method that uses needles for treatment of pain and assorted conditions

Akashic records – a compilation of everything (words, actions, thoughts, deeds) in the past, present, and future

angel cards – Oracle cards depicting angels to access angelic wisdom and guidance. See also: oracle cards.

angel reading – a session during which a Lightworker connects with the angelic realm (through angel cards or other means) in order to answer a question or gain insight for a person or issue

animal communicator – a Lightworker who transmits messages to and from animals

aromatherapy – a form of alternative healing that uses scents, such as essential oils, plants, or other aromatics as treatment

astrologist – one who studies astrology

astrology – the study of celestial bodies (stars, planets, moons, etc.) as it relates to their influence and impact on humans

aura – a field of energy surrounding a living being. A person who can "read auras" can sense colors and other information in this subtle energy field.

auto writing – A method by which a person closes their eyes and begins to write, with the intention of receiving intuitive information or guidance without accessing their conscious brain. Also called psychography or automatic writing.

badassery – the act of doing anything like a boss

body work – a general term used to refer to any kind of physical treatment or healing

calibrate – with regards to pendulum use, this refers to the process of ascertaining one's signs for yes, no, and need more info

candle reading – a form of intuitive reading during which the Lightworker burns a candle for a specified amount of time and then evaluates and interprets certain characteristics of how the candle burned

card reader – A Lightworker who receives and interprets guided information using a special deck of picture cards. See also: oracle cards, angel cards, tarot cards.

chakra – an energy center in the body

chakra balancing – a Lightworking method by which the subtle energy of the chakra centers is opened and cleared. This is helpful to remove stuck energy in one or more chakras, as well as to eliminate energy bottlenecks if a chakra is closed or not properly functioning.

chakra work – a general term referring to any Lightworking method designed to clear, open, and balance the energy of the chakras.

channel (verb) – the act of allowing an energetic being (perhaps one who has crossed over) to speak through you, using your body to channel a message through to the living

channel (noun) – one who channels.

check in – a term used by Lightworkers when they are accessing intuitive messages or verifying the truth or validity of a message. As in, "Let me check in around that and see what I get."

chiropractic – a form of alternative healing by which joints are manipulated either manually or through a device called an "activator" for treatment of a variety of conditions

chiropractor – a person who is trained and licensed to perform chiropractic adjustments

clairaudient – the ability to receive intuitive messages and awareness by hearing (auditory), either out loud or in one's mind

claircognizance – the ability to receive intuitive messages and awareness through an inner knowing and awareness, not necessarily through one of the five senses

clairsentience - the ability to receive intuitive messages and awareness by feeling; the ability to feel subtle energies and the emotions of others. See also: empath

"the Clairs" – a Lightworker term used to refer to the various types of extrasensory perception. See also: clairvoyant, clairsentience, clairaudient, claircognizance.

clairvoyance - the ability to receive intuitive messages and awareness in a visual way, either with the eyes or in the mind's eye

clear (adjective) – able to understand fully; having clarity. Also, the state of being after energy work is complete. "By the end of the session, I was totally clear."

clear (verb) – to remove blocks, doubts, fears, or limiting beliefs by working with the subtle energies. "I'm really stuck around money right now. Can you clear me?"

clearing (noun) – An act of Lightworking by which an obstacle (block, doubt, fear, limiting belief, upsetting emotion, etc.) is removed energetically. "After the clearing, he smiled and felt hopeful for the first time in years."

clearing (verb) – the act of helping a person to get clear through Lightworking

"compare and despair" – a phrase designed to discourage measuring yourself or your results against another person's results, due to the disappointment and frustration that typically stems from such a comparison

coning – a vortex of energy (typically intended for a specific purpose or a specified length of time) created by Lightworkers to convene with earth energy, including entities from the fairy realm

crown chakra – the energy center located at the top of the head (crown). Typically associated with a sense of connectedness to all things.

crystal ball – a clear orb usually made of clear quartz or glass. Crystal gazers can intuit and interpret messages by staring into it.

crystals - naturally occurring rocks and gemstones that contain inherent healing qualities

divine – a word used by Lightworkers as another word for God. See also Source, Spirit, Highest Good, and Universal Energy

doubt – uncertainty

download – a term used by Lightworkers to describe the phenomenon associated with receiving a substantial amount of intuitive information instantaneously, often as an immediate knowing

dowsing – refers to any type of divination that accesses subtle energies to "point" to an answer, such as pendulums, divining rods, or a forked stick used to locate underground water

dream interpretation – the process of analyzing images and sensations from dreams to interpret their hidden meaning in a person's waking life

dry brushing – a physical form of detox by which a stiff, short-bristled brush is rubbed in a downward fashion on the skin. Dry brushing removes dead skin and has an invigorating effect. Some Lightworkers use dry brushing to remove unwanted energy from their field and physical body.

earth angel – a human being who is called at a soul level to bring the high energy of the angels into the human realm here on earth.

Ego – in Lightworking terms, the Ego refers to the aspect of self that seeks self-preservation and the avoidance of pain. Different Lightworkers have different perspectives on Ego, ranging from those who consider it our greatest ally, to those who feel it stymies forward growth and awareness. It likes to be capitalized...no surprise, right?

Ego work – a general term used to describe any Lightworking that involves the Ego

empath – a person who senses and deeply feels the emotions and sensations of other people and sometimes also knows another person's thoughts

empathetic – the ability to sense and deeply feel the emotions and sensations of others

empathic – See: empathetic

energy artist – a Lightworker who creates art. This may be done intuitively, by sensing energy, through guided direction, or by some other means.

energy cleaner – a person who removes negative energy, either consciously or unconsciously

energy healer – a person who conducts energy healings

energy healing – a general term that includes any form of Lightworking designed to restore a person to a state of natural balance, which may be physical, emotional, mental, or otherwise.

energy work - a general term that includes any form of Lightworking that interacts with the subtle energies

energy worker – a person who performs energy work

entity – an energetic being, usually without a physical form or body

ESP (Extra Sensory Perception) – the ability to glean information and awareness through methods beyond the five senses

feng shui – meaning "wind water," this term refers to the ancient Chinese practice of arranging items within a space in order to create harmony

field – in Lightworking, this term refers to a person's entire area of subtle energy, which may include past, present, and future events. "I used my intuition to remove an entity from his field."

ghost – another word for entity.

gift – in Lightworking, this refers to a specific skill or ability as it relates to energy work. "He used his gift to clear the allergy from the child's field."

hands-off healing – a general term that refers to any type of Lightworking that doesn't involve touch. See also remote.

hands-on healing – a general term that refers to any type of Lightworking that requires the healer to physically touch the recipient of the healing. See also body work.

Highest Good – a general term used by Lightworkers to refer to the best interest of all parties involved. "We stopped the treatment, because it was no longer in her Highest Good to continue."

hypnosis – a form of psychotherapy designed to place the patient into a trance in order to allow access to repressed memories or to implant suggestions designed to alter behavior or reverse negative patterns

intuition – an inner knowing or awareness

intuitive (adjective) – possessing an inner knowing or awareness

intuitive (noun) – a person who possesses an inner knowing or awareness

intuitive hit – a term used by Lightworkers to describe a flash of knowing. "I got an intuitive hit to turn left, so I followed it."

intuitive healer – one who conducts energy healings by using his or her intuition

"It is what it is" – a phrase used by some Lightworkers to facilitate acceptance of a certain truth

knowings – a term used by Lightworkers to describe intuitive messages. "My knowings sometimes get me into trouble at work."

Law of Attraction – the Universal principle of "like attracts like." Made popular by the book and movie, *The Secret*.

Lightworker - one who works with energy toward a positive end

Lightworking – a catchall term referring to any kind of intuitive or energy work

massage therapist – an individual trained and licensed in the art and science of manipulating soft body tissues for the purpose of relaxation and healing

medical intuitive – term used to describe a Lightworker who receives information of a physical and health-related nature. "After two months of off and on headaches, I finally saw a medical intuitive who told me my body can't tolerate soy."

meditation – the act of remaining still and focused for a length of time, for the purpose of quieting the mind, receiving intuitive messages, or relaxation

medium – a person with the ability to communicate with entities. Unlike a channel who acts as a mouthpiece for entities to speak directly through, a medium transfers messages to and from entities (usually those who have crossed over), using his or her own voice and personality. John Edward is a well-known medium.

mediumship – the practice of communicating with entities

metaphysics – an abstract principle of philosophy that deals with intangible concepts like time, space, intuition, awareness, etc.

method – a specific way in which Lightworking is conducted

modality – in Lightworking, another word for method

negative entity – an energy being that proves especially difficult or disruptive. "I didn't break that plate. It must have been a negative entity."

numerology – the study of the significance of numbers and their impact on human existence

oracle cards – a divination tool consisting of a deck of cards featuring assorted imagery (and potentially also words and/or numbers). These are cards used to obtain intuitive insight or guidance for a person or around a specific question or issue. See also: angel cards, tarot cards

palm reading – a form of Lightworking during which the lines and markings on the palm of the hand are interpreted to provide information about an individual and/or their future

past life reading – a form of Lightworking during which the Akashic records are accessed in order to reveal and/or heal events from a person's prior lifetimes

past life regression – a variant of a past life reading whereby a person is hypnotized and taken back in time to experience incidents from one of more of their prior lifetimes

pendulum – a weighted object that can swing freely on a string or chain. In Lightworking, a tool for dowsing and ascertaining truth.

protection – in Lightworking, a term that refers to any number of methods intended to prevent present or future harm

protection grid – a form of protection in which crystals are strategically placed in order to create a suggested geometric shape around someone or something "My ex is so cray cray, I had set up a protection grid around my house just to keep him away."

psychic (adjective) – possessing the ability to know information intuitively, or through means other than the five senses or the memory

psychic (noun) – a person who possesses psychic abilities

psychic attack – an event in which one or more negative entities (or a person or persons with ill intent) target a specific person, sending large amounts of adverse energy toward the targeted individual's field, often as a form of revenge or a way to gain the person's attention

psychic healer – another term for a Lightworker

psychic soup – a term used by Lady Roxanna in this book, as a way to describe the development of one's own formula for intuition and healing, as a result of having learned many different Lightworking methods and blending these with one's own discoveries.

psychometry – the ability to gain information intuitively about a person or event by touching an object associated with that person or event

Reiki – a healing modality by which a practitioner channels life force energy and then transfers it to another being, usually through touch

Reiki master – a person who has achieved the Master level of Reiki attunement

remote – in Lightworking, this term refers to healing or energy work that is performed remotely, without being in each other's physical presence

resistance - the energy a person exerts in order to avoid facing some certain Truth about themselves; a refusal to accept

salt bath, also Epsom soak or Epsom bath – a healing treatment during which quality salts (preferably pink, gray, or Epsom) are added to bath water to detoxify the body and cleanse the energy field

scrying – a form of divination in which the inner eye or third eye is used to obtain information and guidance. See also: crystal ball

self-trust - one's ability to value, rely on, listen to, and believe in oneself.

shaman – a term similar to Lightworker; an individual who acts as an intermediary between the seen and unseen realms, typically also with healing abilities

smudge (verb) – in Lightworking, a form of clearing unwanted energy from a person or physical space with the intent to purify, often by using a lit bundle of sage. "She smudges the house every time her mother-in-law leaves."

Source (noun) - a word used by Lightworkers as another word for God. As in "the Source of all energy." See also Divine, Spirit, Highest Good, and Universal Energy

source (verb) – in Lightworking, this refers to the act of creating one's own healing methods or modalities. "I couldn't find anyone to fix this issue for me, so I sourced my own method and got it cleared."

Spirit - a word used by Lightworkers as another word for God. See also Divine, Source, Highest Good, and Universal Energy

spiritual coach – a Lightworker who specializes in guiding individuals to advance on their spiritual path, usually through conversation and verbal exploration

spiritual healer – a Lightworker who restores balance to the subtle energies, clearing obstacles and effecting transformation

subtle energy – the realm in which Lightworkers operate, where life force is sensed in an intuitive fashion, rather than with the five physical senses

tarot cards – a deck of special cards featuring various images, used for divination. The most recognized version is the Rider-Waite Tarot Deck. See also: oracle cards.

technique – in Lightworking, a specific method for accessing and/or affecting the subtle energies

third eye – the chakra located on the forehead, above and between the eyebrows. Typically associated with intuition and psychic awareness. Sometimes referred to as the "inner eye" or "mind's eye."

truth testing - a process used to verify and/or validate information

Universal Energy - a word used by Lightworkers as another word for God. See also Divine, Source, Spirit, and Highest Good

validation – in Lightworking, the process by which intuitive information is verified and certainty is gained.

vibe (noun) – short for vibration. In Lightworking, this refers to assessment of a particular vibration of subtle energy. "Dude, I got the weirdest vibe from that guy." Or, "I get such a good vibe from this apartment."

vibe (verb) – Lightworkers sometimes use this term to refer to an alignment of energy, or vibrational resonance. "When you said that, I thought yes! I'm totally vibing with what you're saying right now."

yoga – a form of body work that revolves around specific physical poses and a focus on the breath.

Resources

Amy Scott Grant's "Spiritual Ass Kicker" books, ebooks, audiobooks, and oracle cards are available on Amazon and on Amy's website:

http://askamyanything.com

Pendulum Mojo: How to Use Truth Testing for Clarity, Confidence, and Peace of Mind

Get Grounded: Learn to Ground Your Energy and Instantly Feel More Calm, Centered, and Peaceful

Spiritual Ass Kicker's Discovery Deck oracle cards

1-2-3 Clarity! Banish Your Blocks, Doubts, Fears, and Limiting Beliefs Like a Spiritual Badass

Patterns of Purpose: Color Your Way to a Better YOU

Terry Robnett's books are available on Amazon:

Wealth Coloring Book: The Secret to Creating More Through Color

Love Coloring Book: Creating More Through Color

Happy Coloring Book: The Secret to Creating More Through Color

Terry's Vitamin B12 energy patches and Vitamin D sunshine patches and liquid drops are available on:

http://InnovativeBalance.com

About the Authors

AMY SCOTT GRANT

Thanks to her highly developed intuition and insatiable quest for human advancement, Spiritual Ass Kicker **Amy Scott Grant** has healed and helped tens of thousands of individuals in more than thirty countries through her speaking, writing, and mentoring. Her extraordinary gift of "Clarity with Hilarity" is no joke: results-based coaching + healing work peppered with a unique sense of humor and a healthy dose of levity.

In September 2013, Amy was inducted into the National Academy of Bestselling Authors and received a prestigious Quilly award at the Golden Gala Awards in Hollywood, California. She was selected as a Thought Leader of the Year Finalist in 2013.

Amy has created a number of successful courses and digital products, including Ripple Magic, HIY (Heal It Yourself): Higher Power Tools, and MindTime™ meditations for kids at KidCentered.com. You can find Amy's writing all over the internet, as well as in the bestselling book *Inspired Marketing* by Dr. Joe Vitale and Craig Perrine; the acclaimed *Chicken Soup for the Soul: Life Lessons for Mastering the Law of Attraction;* the bestseller *Change Agents* with Brian Tracy; and her *Spiritual Ass Kicker Series,* available on Amazon.

Ready to get clear? Connect with Amy directly and claim your free Spiritual Ass Kicker gifts at:

www.AskAmyAnything.com

About the Authors

TERRY ROBNETT, RN

Big strong hugs and hearty laughter are always on tap when you connect with **Terry Robnett.** She is a dynamic, powerful Lightworker, Reiki Master, and Registered Nurse (RN) with a heart of gold. Terry's unique blend of compassion and badassery make her a dynamo Consultant and Life Coach. She is passionate about helping you live into your full potential, so you can make a difference and make an impact.

Terry stands strong in her commitment to transformation, and her passion for health and well being is evident as she leads her clients toward a richer, more fulfilling life. She is the owner of Love-Healing-Balance as well as Innovative Balance, a revolutionary company created to help people take control of their health and wellbeing. Terry is also the author and creator of three manifesting coloring books: *Wealth, Love,* and *Happy*.

"Determination is born out of purpose…knowing that you are gifted for something and this something must be attained. It is never enough to rely on luck or natural talent. You must, above all, believe in yourself, face your goals, and then fight as if your life depended on it."

Discover your purpose and create change in your life now! Visit Terry's website and sign up for her FREE Daily Pumps guaranteed to make you smile:

www.LoveHealingBalance.com

About the Authors

JENNIFER RIPA

Jennifer Ripa is an intuitive life coach and energy healer, yoga and essential oils teacher, painter and writer, and soul whisperer. She focuses her work on unearthing the Divine joyful essence of her clients so they can experience the power of that grace within themselves.

Jen encourages clients to foster a conscious relationship with this potentiality to fuel healing and growth. Her work uncovers counter-productive life and thought patterns and releases them so that clients can choose different models that support growth, transformation, and fulfillment. She can move vast amounts of energy in healing and coaching sessions and engenders the foundation for clients to experience massive breakthroughs.

Jen began her healing journey in 1991, when she traveled to India to study yoga as an undergraduate. Yoga and meditation have been a source of strength and stability throughout her life and provide the foundation for her work. Jen plays healing gongs in sessions with her coaching and healing clients and finds these instruments to have an astounding capacity for change. She also utilizes Reiki and the Rising Star Healing System in her work. Jen employs the restorative qualities of essential oils to assist with liberation and transcendence.

Through her intuitive insights, she accesses physical, mental, emotional, and spiritual wounds, bringing life force energy to allow for profound shifts and healing. Jen works with clients in her Thrivologie healing space in Ridgefield, Connecticut. She also works with clients by phone, Zoom, and Skype. Jen is the artist and creator of the forthcoming tarot deck "Essential Light."

When you connect with Jen, be sure to mention this book, *The Lightworker's Guide to Getting Started,* and save 25% off your introductory session.

www.thrivologie.com

LADY ROXANNA

Through angelically guided readings and personal healing sessions, **Lady Roxanna** will help you raise your vibration and accelerate healing on all levels. Her energy is gentle, and your individualized session will be guided by the angels for your highest good.

Lady Roxanna is a true Southern Belle with a Celtic background: Irish and Scottish. She moved to New Orleans, Louisiana at the age of ten, so you could say she is a Celtic lass with some Southern sass!

After Hurricane Katrina in 2005, Lady Roxanna returned to her spiritual path and later received her Reiki Master attunement in

Bathe, England in 2010. She then received clairvoyant training with Sage Taylor Goddard & graduated as an Intuitive Angelic Miracle (I AM) Healer in 2015. Receiving her certification in Glastonbury, England was a magical experience with Archangel Michael at the ancient Tor (Tower). Lady Roxanna then traveled to Scotland, a land which holds a special place in her heart.

Her certifications include Reiki Master Sensei, Intuitive Angelic Miracle (I AM) Healer & Reader, Money Reiki Grand Master, Soul Retrieval, Certified & Advanced Crystal Healer, and Sacred Activations Practitioner. She is a lifelong student of Feng Shui, Numerology, and Yoga, and she holds Bachelor's Degrees in Nursing and Psychology.

Lady Roxanna works with Archangels Michael & Raphael, the Goddess, Ascended Masters, Reiki Masters, sacred numerology, and crystals, to weave for you a uniquely powerful, magical session-experience that will enhance your energy and your life for years to come.

"I look forward to being of divine service to you if this resonates with your soul!"

Connect with Lady Roxanna and learn more at:

www.LadyRoxanna.com

Just for Fun: How this Book Happened

Yes, we realize this is the type of topic that normally appears closer to the beginning of a book. But that felt a bit self-indulgent to us, so we figured we'd just get right into the helpful content, and let you get to know us first, and then include this at the end to satisfy curiosity.

We (your four authors: Amy, Terry, Jen, and Lady Roxanna) realize being a Lightworker may not have been your first choice for this point in your life. We also realize what it's like to try to resist your calling, and to have it relentlessly pester you until you finally shout, "Alright already! Now show me what the heck that means!" This is something we continue to experience, even today.

When the idea for this book came about, Amy's first thought was, "Ack, really? Don't I have enough on my plate right now?" But the prompt to collaborate with Terry was insistent, and by the time Amy reached out to Terry to say, "Hey, we're supposed to write a book together," Terry's response was, "Yeah, no shit." Goodness knows Terry had plenty of spinning plates of her own. Here's how such an enlightened conversation unfolded in the twenty-first century:

> Amy: "What's this book supposed to be about?"
> Terry: "I dunno. What do you get?"
> Amy: "Nothing. Just that we're supposed to do it."
> Terry: (long sigh)
> Amy: "Yeah, I hear that. Well, let's just sit with it and see what comes up."

There you have it, the birth of a book concept from two overly enthusiastic Lightworkers. We talked again a week later, but still didn't have a clue. Sometimes we think a big part of the journey is learning to roll with it, especially when you're not the one calling the shots (which is not an easy thing for us!).

The next conversation:

> Amy: "Hey, you get any more info about this book?"
> Terry: "Not really. But I tell you what I do notice...so many people are waking up right now and just feeling lost and confused, with no clue what to do next."
> Amy, out of the blue: "Hey, how about 'The Lightworker's Guide to Getting Started'?"
> Terry: "Feels good. Let's check it."
> *Both whip out their respective pendulums to check in.*
> Amy: "I get yeah."
> Terry: "I get hell yeah."
> Amy: "OK, now what?"
> Terry: "I dunno. We've got a title. Let's sit with it again and see what comes up."
> Amy: "I got a lot going on. Wanna give it two weeks?"
> Terry: "Yeah, same here. Talk to you then."

By the way, this is just one of the things you can look forward to as a Lightworker. You'll soon start to attract friends who also understand and explore these mysterious ways, and it can be very reassuring to call up one of them and say, "Hey, guess what?" and have them respond with, "Duh, I got the same thing yesterday."

Neither of us got any more info during the next two weeks. Then, the very morning of the day when Amy and Terry were slated to speak in the afternoon, Amy was out for a walk and suddenly had to sprint home. No, it wasn't the morning coffee kicking in, it was the "bones" of the book coming in, and coming in fast. Breathless, she dropped down in front of her computer and banged on the keys as fast as she could. On that day, this entire book outlined itself, start to finish, each chapter in order. This was a first for Amy, a veteran author.

Then came the hard part.

Once we had the book bones, we were excited to start inviting other Lightworkers to collaborate, so we started reaching out. But we were entirely unprepared for the wall of fear and resistance that met us. Even though we had offered to do the lion's share of the work, to write and publish the entire book, and to provide weekly coaching and guidance to help the collaborating Lightworkers to complete their contributions, we heard every excuse in the book. *I don't have time, I can't afford it, I don't see what I'll get out of it, and couldn't I just write my own book?*

Look, there are plenty of reasons why the majority of people who say they want to write a book don't actually write it. As of this printing, not one of the individuals who declined our invitation to collaborate on this book back in 2017 has published their own book. Not a one! We knew this would be the case, and yet we continued to get stonewalled with nearly every invitation. Several people said yes, but then never followed through. This was frustrating for us because we had so clearly envisioned building a mini-community of collaborative authors.

Finally, we released our expectations, and decided to proceed with this book no matter what. Even if the two of us were the only authors. We knew that Spirit would not let up on us, we knew that this book had to be written, and we knew we were the ones to facilitate its birth. So we made the commitment, and wouldn't you guess, that's exactly when Jen and Lady Roxanna showed up. What a glorious group of four we became! Each week we explored the content of a new chapter and shared our experiences and workshopped our stories, deciding which were of greatest value to offer you. Imagine our surprise and delight to see how very different our four backgrounds and circumstances were, and what a rich tapestry we were weaving to share with you, dearest reader! We could not have imagined a more perfect group of Lightworkers to collaborate with on this book, as we welcome you into our Lightworker community.

This book is living proof that amazing things can be borne from guidance met with initial resistance. Persistence and commitment can carry any Divine idea through to completion. It is fine for you to resist your calling. Continue to work on yourself, to grow and expand, and at some point, that resistance will fall away and your life's work can come forth through you, to make a positive impact on our world.

Even if the process doesn't unfold the way you envision, it doesn't make the journey any less worthwhile.

Happy trails!

Amy & Terry

Come Join Us in the

Lightworker's Guide

Community:

TheLightworkersGuide.com

It's free!

It's fabulous!

It's where YOU belong!